JUMPING OFF THE EDGE RESPONSIBLY

Mastery of Life
By Design

A Surprisingly Simple Method for Eliminating Obstacles in Your Life

BY: DAVID R. VLETAS

Dedication

To our innate gift of contribution in life with generosity and compassion so we may interact with each other. It is also our creativity and imagination which unite us as far as we can continue living in the question, thinking and speaking of great ideas for humanity. This is the source of our vitality, our primary opportunity for unity and global sustainability.

For all the healers who teach and help to evolve our connection with each other. In these times with turbulent waves, I thank you for feeding the planet with love and light, helping to manifest words and energy into form.

TABLE OF CONTENTS

Jumping Off the Edge Responsibly

The Lotus grows in muddy water, and it is this environment that gives forth the flower's first and most literal meaning: Rising and blooming above the murk to achieve enlightenment.

Some of us think holding on makes us strong; but sometimes it is letting go. — Herman Hesse

Introduction
Not Giving Yourself Permission
How Good Can You Stand to Have Your Life Be?

We design ourselves into our experience. As we create our guiding distinctions so we author our lives of greatness or suffering. If you do not give yourself permission to design your life freely, then who will?

I remember thinking, is this what I have been working for? How can I have followed these paths, only to arrive at this place? You are one insight away from a clear path forward. A new realization occurs in an instance and everything is different. Your beautiful idea, yet without taking action, that is all it ever will be, your beautiful idea. You will never know how well you landed if your fear, stress or anxiety kept you from taking the leap and jumping off the edge. Here is to your beautiful landings and learning how to include your fear with confidence! We are all prisoners here of our own method until we are not.

Choosing a designed life is more powerful than your default setting. Your default setting is the one stopping you, that default setting is the one based on fear and control. The red light which only leads to more of the same. You must learn to be courageous again, and lead by creating something new, something sustainable for yourself, the green light. This is your most powerful tool; choosing the green light. This relatively simple dilemma which we are faced with each moment has us be aligned or not.

The lessons learned from your path yielded the valuable life experience you are gifted. It is all a function of moving into the open spaces. Life is about inclusion and integrating as you continue learning the value of choosing well. It is the responsibility of the most awake person in the moment to cut the chain of reactivity.

As you increase your ability to see the people in your life as the teachers which are needed for the important lessons you are here for, you realize how much you have to learn. There is a natural progression to life when we allow it to unfold. When we do not resist it, but rather embrace it and letting it surround us like air and water.

I was hanging out in the coffee shop with my friend Marcel and he was wondering, do you ever notice when you can't stop thinking about something? My response was of course you do, because you can't stop; the thought is in there and needs to come out and be expressed. Let it out dude, just say it. It is mind chatter and at times may become stressful. The question becomes how long can you go on isolating yourself, what is your threshold for pain and suffering. How much longer can you remain involved in the situation before enough is enough? Marcel was procrastinating big time. He knew he was an entrepreneur and an artist since he was a boy. Yet he went into the family business working with his dad and his older brother. You could feel the friction whenever you were around him. It had him and he could not get free. Working in the family construction business was not working for Marcel and the cost was high, and escalating the longer he stayed around as a participant in his family's dream. He had just broken up with his girlfriend and was vacillating in his life. He knew what action to take to free himself yet he was stuck. Being a friend and watching this from the outside is painful; knowing what would free him, and even talking about it with him. You can lead a horse to water, but you can't make him drink. Marcel was like a fine dehydrated stallion standing next to water. His inaction was feeding him what he had always known. Familiarity and safety with a dose of excessive caution is not a rewarding equation for living one's dream. Ignoring your dream while being a participant in someone else dream is a prescription for suffering. Taking action in the direction of your dream gives you freedom and opens up opportunities you never considered possible. A life by design is not your default setting, it is your dream realized.

The distraction of not having connection with your dream and passion, may be the most difficult part. In the end, you are either building something meaningful with satisfaction, joy and fulfillment or not. Procrastination and obsessive mind trash is nothing more than a distraction. It robs you of your creative flow and freedom to live the life of your dreams.

There is something about the rigidity of discipline and following in your father's foot-steps. Discipline has a great purpose until a point then its value becomes suffocating when it is not in alignment with your passion or life dream. Excessive structure and distraction infringes upon your spontaneity and imagination and when it does, discipline needs a rest. You can ride it as far as you can practically, however, reaching the end of its usefulness you must jump off the edge into your inspiration. Touching the challenge of your agility, shifting gears and accelerating into the area of your passion. It is your freedom to connect with others which is an opportunity to assist discipline in not going too far. In Marcel's situation, he has a good life in France living outside of Paris, a secure job and a safe future. However, a problem arises when he is unwilling to jump off into his gift. His dream was moving to England, starting his own business and finding an English-speaking girlfriend to build his life with. Seems simple enough, yet it is not, he was stopped. Creating a life by design guides you in giving yourself permission to follow your dreams, then jumping off responsibly. It is easy to say, yet requires practice becoming confident, doing so in alignment with your optimal aptitudes and connecting with your purpose gives you freedom.

Everything I understand today comes from my desire to experience new people, places, things and ideas. For as long as I can remember I have been a fearless risk taker literally jumping into life, jumping off the edge without regard to the landing. Maturity teaches us how to land beautifully and with a sense of purpose, equally responsibility teaches us how to increase the quality of everything we are.

The problems we have today are a result of the level of thinking we have done so far. These problems will not be solved at that same level of thinking, which created them. We must break the old thinking, the old paradigms and create a new level of thinking if we are to solve them. Albert Einstein –

Reframe. It is in designing forward and using the optimal tools of a life by design which holds your solutions. While using your authentic aptitudes creatively and with style, will have your dream and masterpiece become reality.

Everyone has heard the old adage less is more and simple is better. So true trust in simplicity where less is what works and simple really is optimal. It does not always have to be complicated, learn to know yourself and focus into that gift, then engage it fully, you are home. In Costa Rica they have a saying, Pura Vida, which literally translated means pure life. What could be more-simple, more-pure than this universal grounding principle which I love— Pura Vida!

Chapter 1
Understanding the Problem for Myself
Life Teaches Us When We Can Hear It

I was walking strong and just learning to run, while my curiosity with the water was pulling me towards her. Something about her reflection and the sound's she made, always changing her mood, sometimes soft and smooth and other times stormy and grey. All the colors and textures you could ever imagine with the natural organic scents of life. I was drawn to her, she was where I belonged. I was home by her edge.

I was at the lake with my family and I had been wanting to get to the water, to be in the water every time I saw her. I recognized my chance and bolted down the lawn and out onto the dock, and with cheetah-like speed I leapt off the edge into my home. She was cold and fresh, soft, and holding me in her buoyancy. When I popped up my dad was there plucking me from the lake and into the safety of his embrace. I was squealing with joy. For such an amazing display of athleticism and admiration for the water, I was rewarded with an orange life vest which was attached to a rope and tied to a tree. Within sight of the water, in the shade of the tree, on the green grass, I was trapped, unable to escape my responsibly of jumping off the edge. It is our love of each other and the altruistic gene which gives us that sense of service, the desire to look after and help one another which is one of our greatest gifts. A father's love and a mother's heart are at the core of our universal connection.

I was three years old the first time I saw the Pacific Ocean. We would go to the beach on the weekends leaving early in the morning, and I remember smelling the ocean as we drove down the ramp in Santa Monica, fog still in the morning air. My parents liked going to T's at the #4 life guard tower, we became regulars over the years. This was also the first time I saw waves and people riding them. Imagine people riding waves in the magic water, how could this be? I quickly learned to swim like a fish, having some natural aquatic ability. I felt a sense of belonging and being at peace near the edge of the ocean, diving into her waves. As I grew, practiced and gained experience, I became Finny. My friends thought I was part dolphin.

The Los Angeles County Department of Beaches are the keepers of the treasure. In a sense, this makes the life guards servants of the people and protectors of the ocean. If you have ever been to the beach at T's on the weekend when a good size swell is running, it is a sight to see. The sun is shining, the people are sun bathing and swimming in the ocean, the smell of coconut oil is in the air. The life guards are in full force with their trucks, boats and helicopters, talking on their walkie-talkies, always on the look- out keeping the people safe. It was a Saturday afternoon when I witnessed my first drowning. I was about 7 years old and remember how professional the life guards were. Doing their work with seriousness and a sense of urgency to administer CPR and resuscitate the unconscious boy. They had risked their own lives in the waves to save another. Their skills and sense of service recall the deep respect I have for them. From that day on I have never forgotten their life of service.

You're gonna have to serve somebody —
Bob Dylan

It was a Saturday morning in September and my eighth birthday. I had been begging my dad for a surfboard since I was five. Until then we had been body surfing and riding inflatable matts; those ones you could rent at the beach parking lot. They were blue canvas with yellow rubbery ends. My brother and I played for hours in the waves, catching countless rides all the way in and then paddled back out to catch another. The canvas would rub your belly raw. One of the prices you pay for riding waves. Everything in life has consequences, life lessons. When you experience them enough, you learn. These are the moments in life to build upon and design from, or they become the less than optimal examples, which repeat and dominate your life. It is imperative that you understand their meaning. Learning how to absorb or direct their energy in a creative way brings harmony. Then we have the other side which is something we know we do not want to emulate in any way, these become examples of how not to be or what not to do. Either way life is always teaching us something of value if we are paying close enough attention.

My dad surprised me that morning, when I thought we were just going to the beach. He pulled up in front of Natural Progression Surfboards in the Santa Monica Canyon and we went inside to purchase my first board and wetsuit! It was my eighth birthday and the year was 1968. In the beginning, boards were big. O'Neill wetsuits were thick. Surf board wax smelled great, like coconut and leashes that connect your ankle to the board had not been invented yet.

The 4 main rules of surfing are:

- 1 Don't get hit by your board.

- 2 Don't get hit by someone else's board.

- 3 Don't hit the bottom, and if you do, hit feet first.

- 4 Get Barreled ~ Have fun!

Safety, respect, responsibility, fun and the importance of handling your board so it does not injure you, or another person are extremely important. If you lose control of it or fall, your beautiful board can end up in the pilings, on the rocks or on a reef in pieces. Leashes or leg ropes had not been invented yet. You were very aware of how athletic the sport really is. If you do not have a leash you can't ditch your board. If you want to get to the outside and ride waves you must control your board. You have to be able to paddle out if you wanted to ride waves. Likewise, when you fall you have to be able to swim in to get your board, only to paddle out again to catch another. Oh, surf schools and instructors were only in Hawaii and just beginning to emerge in California. We were on our own.

Today we live in a world with a new surf paradigm, where everyone has a leash. Most new surfers do not know the rules or etiquette, including surf instructors. Yes, some surf instructors do not know how to swim and they also ditch their boards because they have a leash. The word chaos is what comes to mind. Surfboards are projectiles, when they are ditched into someone's path. Counting on the leash to save them, sets a dangerous precedent, because leashes do snap. There is a natural progression to surfing, as with any endeavor or skill in life. It is a rite of passage and dues to pay. The learning curve is not an easy one, but the rewards of riding waves or achieving your designed goals are well worth it.

Again, we are back to consequences and life lessons. What are you designing and how bad do you really want it? Being mindful to what you are building and your ability to change quickly are your adaptation advantages. These learned skills become increasingly important in building or designing anything as your systems become more complex. Being resolute does not serve us. It is the development of our cognitive agility which does. Resolute is the old paradigm of right and wrong. Unfortunately, most people are still living in this world; stuck with this old reasoning and its restrictive meanings. The root of all problems is being stuck with a meaning or interpretation which is not valid or accurate and has outlived its' usefulness. Sadly, most people do not recognize when this is happening to them.

Thankfully, you don't have to live in that world any longer if you don't want to. The answer is to simply remove your self-imposed restrictions. Well, that is not as easy as it sounds. Especially if you do not know how to remove the program, and if you don't realize a program is running. Shiza! Houston, we have a problem. It is your life by design and using specific tools which gives you the ability to generate new interpretations which free your creativity and imagination, and improves your connection to others. Creating a life by design releases you from your old ideas and limitations. A life by design becomes your practice and your path to freedom.

The ocean is a great master and my beautiful mentor. The surfing metaphor is applicable to all the domains of ones' life. I started noticing early on how important it is to pay attention and connect the dots. Life is experiential and has its own momentum which can earn you the perfect ride, or have you crash and tumble.

This result is depending on your experience, or preparation to be present in the moment. Our learning is a function of participation which requires many lessons. Most of these lessons result in not achieving the desired outcome. Learning to endure the impact zone earns you the opportunity to surf the beautiful waves. You must get to the outside if you are to participate and give yourself the chance to catch one and ride her energy. Persistence and tenacity of purpose are key in any realm you wish to master. It's your focus in the area of your optimal aptitude and skill set, while using your creativity and imagination, which has you be free.

I was in my senior year at Santa Monica High School (1978). These were amazing times full of learning, surfing, skating boarding pools, and drainage ditches and speed runs down the canyons. It was the world after Viet Nam, before AIDS and with the best music ever being made. It was a time of excess, bonfires and partying at the beach. It got the best of me.

It was a spectacular crash. The last thing I remember hearing was "let's see how fast we can go!" It was a rainy night in January and we were driving north on PCH after a Saturday night in Santa Monica. The collision was head on, going about 70 mph. There was a camper shell that had a boot which connected the back to the front seats. I was sitting in the back with Matt. I remember Robin Trower's "Bridge of Sighs" playing loud as Nelson hydro-planed his pickup truck across the emergency lane and into the fast south bound lane. Jeff was sitting shot gun. We were in front of the Jetty, across from the Sun Spot Bar, when the impact occurred. Miraculously, no one was severely injured or killed. Apparently, we all still had some work to do here. Life is special and we are much greater than we realize. A lot of life is about remembering and gaining deeper access to our collective consciousness so we may help others, being of service, to our brothers and sisters, connecting the dots and forwarding our optimal contribution.

I remember being out of my body in the emergency room at Santa Monica Hospital watching on. I was observing them from above hovering around the room. They were checking my body and talking about how I was going to be. I was released within a day and was on my way home to recover from a concussion they said I would have for six months. I was pretty much road rash all over my body and my chest was compressed so severely I would not do a push up for quite some time. There was the issue of would I graduate or have to repeat? My parents were getting divorced. My dad was an attorney and a good provider. He loved us and showed affection naturally. However, he had a drinking problem and had moved out with his girlfriend. My mom was battling her own obstacles and having a difficult time with her divorce. That being said, she is an amazing woman and incredibly generous and loving. My older brother was away living his life, and my baby sister was a mess. In the meantime, my mom's best friend was nursing me back to health, soothing me, caring for me, bringing me back to life. Without Roxanne, it would have been hell. She was my haven and my only safe place. After three week's I was back to school and managed to graduate with my class in June.

I really loved surfing more than anything and I wanted to move to Hawaii and surf the North Shore, settle in for the summer and be there for the first winter swells to arrive. This was not to be. At this point I was not ready, still too young and without enough life experience to know the difference. I was too naive and impressionable to follow my heart. I was still influenced by and listening to the protective reasonableness of the adults who were advising me. They were giving the best guidance they were capable of, operating from the paradigms they were influenced by. Yes, it was the familiar story most of us heard; go to college, cut your hair, and get a real job. Life lessons and experience are what happen along the way. We are all awakening at our own pace and ability to access who we really are. It is the remembrance of our connection to each other which allows us to awaken more quickly, closing our consciousness gap. Our souls have already arranged a meeting before our bodies ever see each other. I believe we have all been here before, and we do not remember how to access what it is we forgot we knew. Here is to regaining access to remembering!

There are many ways we learn. One is emulating what we like and respect, designing from there, and moving forward to something innovative or improved. Another is not emulating what we don't like, while defining what does not work about the system and not doing that. Creating a life by design shows you how to distinguish quickly and make optimal choices. I'd like to interject with a point relating my son, Alex, who would not be born for another 14 years. Early on, when Alex was in his young teens, he displayed an aptitude for and joy of performing. Alex loved to act, sing and dance, and he had talent. Alex was an actor waiting to happen. Fortunately, as a result of my life lessons, I recognized this and never gave him the "go to college, cut your hair and get a real job" speech. Alex got a green light to pursue his passion because it was his gift and aptitude. Squelching this in any way with cultural reasonableness would cause harm to the trajectory of his life by design, interrupting the natural development and authentic contribution he has to make. Alex is amazing and on his way to becoming a fine actor.

Escaping Los Angeles, going to college, cutting my hair and getting a real job:
Moving to Colorado was a really good experience for me. In a sense, life propels you in the direction of your choosing, and to the degree of your focus on what you are building

or the life lessons you have yet to learn. I had a strong aptitude for advertising and marketing, however, this would not come to be, at least in a career sense. The cultural influences and the advice of my counselors had influenced my intuitive judgement again and I would not choose optimally due to my cultural reasonableness. I had bought the North American trap again even though I knew better, there was a part of me that knew the ocean was still calling me home. I was awakening slowly.

After my first semester at Regis College in Denver I found another passion of mine, it was my love of Geology. When I was a young boy, my maternal grandfather, French, would take us hunting and fishing in the summer, and at Christmas, when we would visit family in Abilene, Texas. I was about six when he planted the geology seed. We were sitting on a limestone bluff in west Texas overlooking a ravine where the deer would pass. He was talking to me about the terrain and the rocks explaining the different colors, textures and about fossils. He explained that these rocks we were looking at had been in the ocean over a hundred million years ago. In fact, they were once living creatures. I said, "No way! really?" and he insisted "Yes!" I was in awe. These were beautiful seeds he planted that day, and ones which sprouted roots.

I would go on to attend the Colorado School of Mines in Golden, and ultimately graduate from the University of Texas in Austin with a BS in Geology and a minor in Petroleum Engineering. I briefly considered getting a higher degree yet opted out for life experience. After graduation, I had several interviews and an opportunity to go back to Colorado and work with a company employing over two hundred people. I had the concern of being cubby holed as a company geologist and not learning the overall business in which we were engaged. That business was exploration and providing the world with energy. We were finding, producing and selling oil and natural gas. I also had the opportunity to go and work in Texas with a small independent company, where I could learn the oil business and gain the experience I needed to eventually start my own business. After three years of working there that is what I did. I was independent. It was 1988. Having been land locked in Colorado, Wyoming and Texas, the ocean was always calling me, and several times a year I would make time to go ride waves with her. I also had a great love of the mountains and enjoyed their energy and beauty; the grounding force of mountainous geology and its rawness in my face. My love of and connection to the mountains and skiing in the Rockies and especially the Tetons are strong, however, they are secondary to my ocean home, belonging by her edge.

We are fully accountable and responsible for generating an interpretation that works optimally in any situation which forwards the motion of our contribution. It is our ability to change and adapt quickly which allows us access to our optimal aptitudes, creativity, imagination, and our connection with the collective consciousness.

By mindful focus and practice you increase your ability to be present to the gift of life, navigating in and out of her different domains, unrestrained in your ability to love.

Becoming your own best friend and developing your connectedness in this regard is a practice of mastery which grants you greater access to our universal knowledge and wisdom.

I had been working as an independent consulting geologist now for about a year and a half, when my first experience with professional coaching at this level occurred. It has had a profound impact on me, and continues to be the most interesting thing I do to this point. Integration of body, mind and soul and practicing to build my own level of mastery and sharing it with others in all my interactions and across all the areas of my life is inspiring. I continue to awaken my desire for the remembrance of our connectedness and share these universal truths with others. What a fun ride being of service in this way.

It is a very satisfying and fulfilling experience; sharing knowledge and this expression of joy.

Carolyn invited me to go out one evening so I could meet some of her friends she had been doing some work with. I was super excited to be invited and was attracted to her immediately. There was something different about her that I could not describe. It was more about the way she was acting that was unique to her beauty and differed from the other women I had been around. I did not know what it was all about, but I wanted to be involved in what they were learning. It was a Tuesday evening in Austin Texas when she took me to an Introduction to the Forum. I registered that night and I was excited about life in a way I had never experienced before. In this short time, I had learned more about thinking vs. having thoughts and generating new perspectives, distinctions and paradigms than any other period in my entire life. I knew then why I wanted to help people put this to use in their lives.

This conversation, these simple distinctions, are what is missing in the public-school system. How could something as simple as this not be included in our primary education? I was excited for the new information and also felt a sense of betrayal for not having been taught this before. How could this be? Not teaching you how to think for yourself and being powerful so you may help yourself and share it with others. This is the opposite of service, intentionally denying valuable information and helping your fellow man, or did they simply not know any better, being trapped in their own archaic paradigm?

I do believe it is important to make this point, and I want to introduce the distinction now. It is the intention of this book to address what I have termed the North American Trap, cognitive dissonance in action, or our collective unconsciousness. **Cognitive Dissonance** is when people are resolute and have core beliefs which are black and white. When they encounter information or evidence that disproves those beliefs. Because of their resolute the new information or evidence cannot be believed or accepted. It creates an experience that is very confronting. Often people believe it is critical to protect their core beliefs. They become delusional and will rationalize, defend, justify or ignore anything which does not agree with or support their belief. This is distinguished from the North American dream, **De Cognitive Dissonance** and our collective consciousness, representing our maximum creativity, imagination and paradigm generating tool. This is the freedom we have fought for. It is something I have investigated in great detail while designing courses of action for myself, with clients and corporations who use these types of distinction, to their creative advantage, in forwarding programs and a life by design. Those ideas and opportunities help humanity. They build on our connectedness and unity in the area of sustainability. We will revisit this later on when we begin to cross the bridge and jump off some edges together.

I would go on to participate in almost every course they had over the coming years. In about two years I became a coach in some of their programs and ultimately an Introduction to the Forum Leader. Having worked in many capacities, programs and areas with thousands of people. I have been coaching and mentoring individuals and corporations ever since, while advancing my work in the energy sector and integrating coaching into those relationships. I am also a Strategic Intervention coach and continue my training and development to this day in the Master Level Mentoring Program with Mark and Magali Peysha. Mark and Magali have extraordinary life designing skills and help thousands of people in many different ways. They are amazing coaches and mentors. I am fortunate to be working with them as I deepen my practice daily.

In 1993, I had the pleasure of working with a client, a young woman named Mary, who had just broken up with her boyfriend, and was returning back to college for another degree. As it turns out she was pregnant and did not know it yet. Separated relationships involving a child are normally difficult, and often times they are heartbreaking. The damage done to children, as a result of spouses or parents disagreements, and the differences in regard to their inability to get past problems pertaining to the unresolved issues from their past, can be very destructive. These types of relationships may take years to become civil, if ever. Often times the courts become involved and the state may decide the outcome of the child.

In this instance, Mary had wanted to get married and her boyfriend did not want to be married. Often people will submit to pressure from their families, and the "do the right thing" conversation regarding a pregnancy out of marriage. "Be a man, take responsibility for your actions and make her an honest woman." This is the status quo and rarely, if ever, an optimal solution or beneficial strategy for the child. A consensual relationship out of love, without constant arguments and fighting between the parents creates a more favorable environment for a child to be raised in.

After telling her then boyfriend she was pregnant, there was a long pause. The relationship was good enough for honest communication but not great by any means. As a result of speaking with and coaching both parties we designed a workable solution, a life by design, where the following occurred.

They came to mutually agree and understand that because she was pregnant was not an optimal reason to get married. I had them design a possible future in which it would make sense for them to get married at some point later on. What they came up with was, being in love, wanting to spend the rest of their lives together, wanting to have more children intentionally were reasons to get married. I had them leave room to add any new reasons if they thought of any which might come up later. They agreed to be in communication about how they were feeling and what they were thinking. They were engaged in creating a life by design and did not allow their fear of responsibility or having to do something society was dictating make their choices. This was now an expression of their creativity and imagination focused in the direction of what was optimal for their child's future. They were aligned.

We also spoke about the possibility of abortion and had a paternity test done just in case, although she insisted that he was the father. Nevertheless, it eliminates any lingering doubts having done so. It was agreed that having or not having the baby was her right and that he would support any decision she made. She elected to have the baby and when he was informed he was a little bit in shock. However, after speaking with him about their life design choices again, he came to see it was an opportunity to embrace having the child. He came to realize and design a life where he would be the father 100%. He saw that being accountable and responsible works in raising their child. He promised that she could count on him to always make his monthly payments and to help in the raising of their child in any way for mutual benefit to their and the child. They came to understand and realize that their differences now or in the future would have no bearing on the optimal wellbeing of their child. They agreed to parent in a way that had everything focus on and revolve around the well-being of their child and to not let their personal differences interfere with that priority. Separation of domains is powerful. It allows clarity in and focus of purpose.

Both parties were very pleased with this agreement and though they never married each other, remain good friends today while co-parenting their son. I can hardly imagine a better result. I do not believe they have had two cross words in their relationship since. This is the power of a life by design.

I was coaching a young man who was experiencing burn out in his career. Manny had grown up in the US and was having a difficult time coping with stress in his job, social life and his failing marriage. His messed-up life was starting to express itself in his deteriorating health. He was experiencing chest pains. He was starting to put on weight due to his waning interest in going to the gym or eating properly. He was in the North American Trap, and it was killing him.

After distinguishing his stories about his job, relationships and marriage, he saw how the meaning he had given them was not optimal nor factual and was at the root of the problems he had created. Not only that, it occurred to him that he had been defending the meaning he gave to those issues and even manufacturing evidence to justify them. (Cognitive Dissonance)

We designed many other possible outcomes and interpretations about what had happened. We discussed how the different meanings he made up affected how he felt, depending on the meaning he assigned them. Once he came to realize he was in charge of owning and creating his reality, he had a new-found sense of confidence and freedom to move forward. He resolved those past events which had been stressing him out. Wow! You could see the light come on when he got it. He was free.

And we were just getting started, unfortunately his marriage did not survive, he and his wife were separated and she filed for divorce. My client was an attorney practicing real estate law, and he hated it. He knew he did not want to practice law after two years of law school, yet he stuck with it out of a sense of obligation to his family and a false sense of pride. This is a tricky one to break free of, he had a "should' and 'ought to be" conversation about following through in life and becoming a good lawyer because his father and his grandfather were lawyers. He had never really identified with himself or considered seriously what he loved; what his passions were. I remember kidding him about it and being playful because when he spoke of it seriously it made him want to cry. He was very angry about not having been supported by his family in his passion for martial arts as a child. Upon re-discovering the importance of his childhood dreams and using metaphor work we designed an amazing and practical plan to assist him in implementing his new life which we were designing, a life by design. Using the tools of life by design and

Jumping off the Edge Responsibly, we created his new way forward. He had always liked sports in school and enjoyed being outdoors. He was not interested in wearing a suit and tie ever again and was ready to Jump off the Edge Responsibly. He just did not know into what, or where, and he even had considerations about how. However, he was willing to design it. If you do not give yourself permission to, then who will? He loved to swim and be in the sun and during high school he was a runner. After two more session's he was gaining clarity and within the month a practical plan was devised and he was ready to Jump off the Edge Responsibly! Manny is currently living in Panama where he is a personal trainer and selling real estate, and he has a new wife and a beautiful baby boy. He is happy, fulfilled and understands how to design an optimal life. Cheers to their beautiful landing!

One of my edges, with a beautiful landing, is living in Costa Rica since 2003. Managing my wellbeing is the main priority (body, mind and soul), and creating balance newly every day so my life is optimized to make my best contribution. I am working with clients and forwarding their process of a life by design. I am always learning and gaining access to new insights and distinctions daily. My internal conversation is hilarious and elevating. I am my own best friend and I am coachable! I am surfing every day and forwarding our sustainability for the planet (physically, socially, culturally and consciously). Enjoying sunset walks on the beach and living with my partner Kathryn, and sharing life with our dog Mango. Mango is amazing, and a rescue from the streets of Esperanza. He is one of the best souls I know. My work at the Costa Rica Wellness Institute is life changing. Having a coaching practice is both humbling and fulfilling. I am honored to help people redesign their lives optimally so they can live their dreams. One of my commitments is designing a less hydrocarbon dependent society, and being the bridge to a more sustainable future. I always knew I would find my way home to the ocean. Here is to designing your way forward and living your dreams!

Synchronicity and our intimate connection to our collective universal consciousness. A cosmic sign you are headed in the right direction. To the degree we are in alignment with our ultimate contribution is the degree to which we are connected. —Carl Jung

Everybody is a genius. But, if you judge a fish by its ability to climb a tree, it will live its whole life believing it is stupid. - Albert Einstein

Chapter 2
A Life Time of Possibilities
Choosing Poorly Until We Learn

In total darkness, we are all the same. It is only our knowledge and wisdom which separate us. Do not let your eyes deceive you.
—Janet Jackson

In certain way's we are all evaluating our lives to see what's next, and how we can best move forward in the direction of our passions. It is in the meaning which you give to the events of your life, the assigned significance, which either controls or frees you. The ironic thing about the assigned meaning is, why not assign meanings that free you as your normal course of action? Why allow the default setting, those controlling meanings, to take hold in your life, creating the obstacles

hindering the realization of your dreams?
Take your life back now. Physically, socially culturally and spiritually you have managed to complicate simple things in your life which hinder your opportunity for moving your ambitions forward. A high-quality life is a function of your best understanding. The implementation of practical steps in alignment with your unique talents and gifts. Now that is all good, when you are able to relate to it in that way, however, a flaw arises when you do not have this understanding, and act as if the obstacles you assigned meaning to are real. I am sure you have been designing your life for quite some time now and with varying degrees of success or desired outcomes, sometimes productive and other times not so productive. You know a lot about building something inspiring and realize the challenge

of the endeavor. You may say, if it were easy everyone would do it. You might find yourself saying this frequently when you are in the middle of implementing a new solution. There is nothing easy about it, life is by your own choosing and by your own design. You alone are fully accountable and responsible for what you have done and made of yourself. Uncovering your unique purpose in life is a gift worth seeking. You are here to remember just that, and share it in the world in such a way that leaves you inspired for more. Those times when you experienced balance and flow, and things came together naturally, you were aligned with your purpose and achieved results. So how do you create a way of doing this repeatedly in your life? It is important to evaluate and acknowledge those things which are your stops. By defining them and bringing them into the light of day they lose their power to be controlling in the way they once were.

Perhaps it is your social and cultural distractions and the resulting inaction, which leads you to not being present in your life and influencing your ability to follow through. This is a key piece of what has you stuck, being isolated and giving you a feeling of not being connected. Yet, you persevere knowing that you are under performing, wondering, how is this going to turn out? How is this going to change? This has got to change. I have got to do something to alter my course. Your problems seem complicated and progress seems slow, sometimes coming to a stand-still. Feeling as if you made a mistake.

Your stops; aka obstacles, rob you of what you say you want and are the main consideration of your infinite opportunity to designing your way out of the muck and into the direction of your dreams. The cost of being addicted to distraction on society is in the billions of dollars annually, yet this is the least of our worries. The amount of stress, lost intimacy in all our relationships, poor health, not enough self-love or any kind of love for that matter and not being engaged in life is a lacking and tragic loss. Perhaps the biggest cost of all is not having followed your vision, not building your intuition and making your dream come true. Spending the rest of your life wishing that you had, only if you had done…? You are coming to the realization you are not getting any younger, and questioning how are you going to put all your life experience to good use. Unless you do something soon, this thing will own you and continue controlling your life.

This book is very good news for you. It is going to advance your life and alter your perspectives. Your life is going to change by your own design.

These are some of the opportunities to put in what's missing while editing out what is causing you friction, resistance, drag and diverting you to procrastination mode and your chronic distractions. One of the key components necessary to producing extraordinary results and a life you love is you remaining aligned and focused on your purpose. Consistent behavior creates consistent outcomes, so aligning with yourself is key.

Designing your life is the ultimate opportunity and one which requires all of your attention and utilizing all of your resources to the best of your ability. What you know about yourself, your strengths, aptitudes and optimal skills is critical in implementing what it is you say you want to achieve. One of the beautiful things in life is designing it, taking risks and experiencing new things. You have come to this book for a reason and it is no mistake you are here to obtain some information regarding the improvement of your life's trajectory. An increase in the quality, satisfaction and fulfillment of your life for yourself, your family, your career, and the contribution you are here to make to those in your life.

You are not one to shy away from opportunity when it comes knocking. There are strengths in numbers and we are better together than alone. A coaching relationship gives you an advantage, and is an important choice and a distinct benefit you give to yourself when you take on being- coached. You already are a high functioning person who realizes the value of this type of experience and relationship. One example in this regard I enjoy sharing with people is what one of my first coaches, Elaine, shared with me about Olympic athletes. The difference between athletes who bring home the Gold, Silver and Bronze medals and the rest of the field is the quality of their relationship to mentoring or coaching. It is their ability to accept and incorporate mentoring or coaching into their integrated life by design. Managing your life creatively and with style, especially in the face of transitions is powerful. World class athletes come face to face with the wall and they must breakthrough repeatedly if they are to accomplish their goals.

The same is true for my friend Marcel. He was facing the challenge of setting out on his own in the direction of his dream, and independent from family influence, while remaining a loving and supportive brother and son. We are all facing obstacles. This is your access to having an amazing life you love and one that gives you energy! The time is now to release your obstacles, and flip your green light switch.

The art of life is beautiful and intricate and is enhanced by the dance between risk and responsibility. Using the eight steps of life by design is a surprisingly simple practice focusing on the specific areas of your life which are most important to you. Gaining experience using the tools and focusing on your optimal aptitudes and passions is enriching and satisfying. You will discover in our dialogue a balance across many boundaries. As you define the most important areas of your life, you will begin to design your plan for action. As we formulate this uniquely to your specific circumstances you will begin to use strategies that uncover why your productivity was stuck in certain areas. Some people find it overwhelming to be held accountable and responsible for doing what they say. Then also being held accountable to deliver on their promise and be on time. For example, if you have a meeting with your employer, client or a friend and you see you are going to be late, what works is giving them a call before you are late and saying, hi, I am going to be 30 minutes late, so I wanted to see if you could make that work?

Otherwise, let's schedule another time now, when we can have our meeting and get together then? Confirm and keep your appointment. Basic communication and respect are base requirements for being accountable and responsible. Without them we are at a great disadvantage of contributing our gift or maintaining close relationships. If your friends or employer can't count on you then who can? We earn trust and respect, being accountable is key to both.

It has been an adventurous journey getting to where I am now so that I can share with you the things you are about to access. From my time working as a coach and my inquiry into what it is to be a human being, I have experienced how quality of life, satisfaction and fulfillment are linked to designing one's life and implementing a specific plan. Your ability to distinguish new tools and perspectives will give you the insights you are seeking. In the process, all of your relationships benefit greatly as you practice these new skills and increase your ability to design specifically in the area of your inspiration, while utilizing your optimal aptitudes and skill sets.

As you increase your advantage from continuing to learn new information, knowledge, and skills, while collecting experience and seeking wisdom in tandem with a coaching relationship your progress will accelerate. Choosing to commit and invest in your own life in this way is powerful. It is in the committing the actual act of investing in yourself when things will begin to change. Hesitancy only brings more of the same. The remaining pieces are equally important. The practice of designing your life while generating new tools and perspectives, and their practical implementation into your life, becomes both your opportunity and your challenge. Ultimately, the greatest satisfaction and fulfillment comes from being able to share with the people in your life your new life by design. People will notice something has changed about you, as your focus and purpose begin driving you with a new sense of happiness and joy. You are no longer running your life from the default setting.

The journey is intriguing and playful, applying yourself to serious issues, however, not taking yourself too seriously. This process is very focused and full of insights and distinctions on how to connect the dots and use the tools constructively in your life. The eight steps of life by design will guide you on your journey to mastery in your life. It is important to embrace the process and enjoy the ride. Trusting your practice to produce the results is key to increasing your level of mastery moving forward. Significant progress, benefits and advantages do occur quickly when applying new distinctions. Field testing and note taking are important too, as you will be designing your own tools and distinctions as you grow. To the degree you apply yourself to this process, is the degree to which you will generate greatness in your life by design.

Your practice will have your obstacles and stops no longer obstructing and controlling you. The reasons you have for being stopped, those normal things in your life which have restricted you, will no longer hinder you from achieving your goals. Once you begin applying these tools, your life will be altered.

As you begin to grow and improve in your abilities you move closer to your realized purpose. Your ability of being accountable and responsible for generating the results of your designed life is in direct proportion to your relationship with being open. Your willingness to integrate the interactions from that dialogue into the design of your life also affects your results. On the other hand, to the degree you lack the commitment to being focused or being in action and developing a level of mastery in designing your life, you will likely experience more of those stops, issues, and obstacles you wish to eliminate. A life by design has you adapt all those issues in your favor, in the direction of your satisfaction.

It is a common misconception in life that since you have read the book you believe you have mastered the materials. Some people have photographic memories and retain information that way, or even experientially (an actual recollection of what happened without distortion) however, for most of us this is not the case. You probably have to learn new material by re-reading, journaling or experiencing it by repetition, practice or perhaps some visual method, or whatever the case may be for your unique learning style. The point being, just because you have read something you thought was interesting does not equate to developing mastery in that area. You must remain open and be willing to adapt, while making the contributions you have to make to those in your life. Reading the Kung Fu manual does not make you a Kung Fu Master.

It has been my pleasure helping thousands of people break through their obstacles while educating, inspiring and empowering them to design amazing outcomes for themselves their families, businesses and communities. It is the intention of this book to share with you some of the materials I have created and used over the years as well as the new distinctions I continue to generate with my clients and for myself. This work is very powerful in its simplicity and its mind friendly nature. We will define your optimal aptitudes and passion and then focus on building from there, improving your skills and procedural implementation, while diminishing and eliminating your stops.

Try not to become a person of success, but rather try to become a person of value. — *Albert Einstein* (20th Century / Einsteinian Universe)

There is no trying, only doing. —*Yoda* (21st Century Jedi Master / Quantum Universe)

This is a great playful example of why change is so critical and your ability to change or adapt quickly is an advantage you give to yourself. Philosophy evolves into Metaphysics and the Einsteinian Universe gives way to the Quantum Universe with its advanced mathematics and physics, mainly due to technological advances that proved some of Einstein's theories (among others, which allowed for the evidence to prove models that validate them for now). This leads to new insights, distinctions and paradigms, which make the old ones the example of what once was believed. The continuing cycle of this theory keeps you increasing your creativity, imagination and freedom. Out of this falls your ability to connect deeper with our universal truths and remembering your access to the collective consciousness and our infinite source of energy wisdom and freedom. - The synchronicity is beautiful.

This book covers a lot of ground quickly and repetition is important to break through from concept to experience. Through repetition you have the opportunity to say something or see something in a slightly different way allowing for subtle insights which often lead to creative new distinctions and even life changing paradigms. I look forward to sharing with you and jumping off some edges together. Please hold on and be open to the process, this is an amazing journey you are about to take.

Life is either a daring adventure or nothing at all — Hellen Keller

The Eight Steps of Life by Design

- 1 **Owning Your Cognitive Dissonance (CD):** Coming to grip with what is accurate to the best of your ability. This is the practice, as you develop your mastery, where everything opens up, differentiating what is so and what is not so. Observe the trap, you'll learn where all your obstacles come from. They live here. Evaluate the meaning of your-stories. Understand your collective **un**consciousness. Being out of alignment is the default setting.

- 2 **De Cognitive Dissonance (DCD):**
Recognition of your power to create and
design. Differentiating your obstacles and
removing your stops, by generating new
interpretations which align with your
optimal aptitude and abilities to propel you
forward into your purpose and maximum
contribution to humanity. Your new life by
design awaits. **S**uffering **I**ndex **G**ap **(SIG)**
is the time it takes to go from **CD** to **DCD**.

- 3 **Cognitive Agility (CA):** Practicing **CD,
DCD** and **SIG** distinctions. Getting your
hands on the wheel, beginning to generate
your own insights, distinctions and
paradigms. Your creativity, imagination
and confidence are increasing. **This is
where a life by design starts to take off!**

- 4 **Integrating your Practice** into your
body, mind and soul. It is all about

optimizing your system, becoming your best friend and increasing your-self value and love. This is where managing your well-being becomes your priority so you are nurtured and have the ability for maximum contribution. Being healthy, balanced and present allows for flow to happen.

- 5 **Defining your Purpose:** By using the tools from your practice thus far, we explore your passions and dreams further to forward an optimal life by design strategy and have a practical look over the edge. We consider the logistical issues and prepare for a beautiful landing.

- 6 **The Dimensional Bridge:** Recognition of where you are on the bridge allows for fine tuning your life by design and making adjustments, while being accountable, responsible and anticipating the unknown. You are fully aware of your purpose, your connection with the collective consciousness and the importance of your contribution to humanity.

- 7 **The Pause Principle Mastery of Mindfulness:** You are on the bridge grounded and including your fears with confidence. Standing on the edge you are **Jumping off the Edge Responsibly** into your gift.

- 8 **Elevate your Practice of Mastery:** Continuing your integration while increasing your awareness and ability to access the synchronicity and execute on your purpose. Sharing with others your growth and practice, being of service, preparing to jump off the next edge.

Chapter 3 / Step One
Cognitive Dissonance
A Look at the Problem
All of Your Obstacles
Live Here

- **Step 1 Owning Your Cognitive Dissonance (CD):** Coming to grip with what is accurate to the best of your ability. This is the practice, as you develop your mastery, where everything opens up, differentiating what is so and what is not so. Observe the trap, you'll learn where all your obstacles come from. They live here. Evaluate the meaning of your stories. Understand your collective **un**consciousness. Being out of alignment is the default setting**.**

Cognitive Dissonance (CD): is designed into people's lives in one way or another and to one degree or another. When people are resolute and have core beliefs which are very strong and they encounter information or evidence that may work opposite to those beliefs, the new information or evidence cannot be believed or accepted. It creates an experience that is very confronting, called **CD**. As I mentioned before, people believe it is critical to protect their core beliefs. They become delusional and rationalize, defend, justify or ignore anything which does not agree with or support the core belief.

An archaic paradigm, such as the earth is flat is one such example. There was a time when the new paradigm of a round earth generated an experience of extreme discomfort in those who could not accept that perspective or **CD**. Just forty years ago we would look at pictures of a static solar system on a page or a poster as if it were accurate, the planets revolve around the sun. Yet today we watch a video of a spiraling solar system (vortex) hurling through the universe on a trajectory at thousands of miles per hour. Another good example is the bag phone to present day apple like products. Also, mechanical watches to digital watches, these different paradigms were revolutionary at the time and the people in control never realized it and even denied it. We live in a digital paradigm. It is happening in computing now with the new quantum paradigm. We've gone vertical on the exponential slope, it is happening every day all around us, and we are missing it all the time. Now, no one is capable of keeping up with every new distinction, however, we are capable of generating new ideas which lead to new paradigms in the areas we specialize in. This can have a big impact and be of tremendous service to the world and humanity. Giving up being right, your reasons and justifications when they do not serve your purpose optimally, elevates your creativity. Now perceive the next best outcome giving yourself freedom to design obstacles out of your life while implementing these new ideas.

Burning Down the House (Of the old Paradigms)
— David Byrne and The Talking Heads

We are living in amazing times and as the advancement and complexity of information and technology continue to accelerate (the approaching Artificial Intelligence singularity), it is critical that you remain engaged. You will learn new tools and ways of staying informed while applying your skills in the areas of your optimal aptitudes. It is your responsibility to dispel information which you once believed was useful or even true which is no longer valid or accurate. This allows you to adapt quickly and remain relevant, otherwise you are in danger of becoming increasingly under performing in the contribution you are capable of. There is someone in your life who needs you to make the contribution you are here to make to them and others. Don't let your obstacles prevent that achievement.

Your own **CD** is just a story, a fabrication, something made up, who's meaning is no longer valid. It is a universal hindrance to accelerating your adaptation. To the degree you can recognize and own it, your **CD** will disappear and cease to have any power over you. The **S**uffering **I**ndex **G**ap **(SIG)** is your personal threshold to self-inflicted pain and suffering. The **SIG** is the amount of time it takes you to go from **CD** modality to **DCD** modality. The longer you hold on to old patterns and stories, those entrenched beliefs, rules and reasons, the larger your **SIG** is. They don't serve you, yet, you tolerate them and even defend them, granting them space in your life. They are the cause of not experiencing happiness, satisfaction, joy, and love in your life. Until you handle this, all those great dreams, ideas and your grand aspirations are not likely to ever be achieved, until you understand and apply this. If you do manage to generate some greatness and achieve a high level of accomplishment it will not be ultimately satisfying or fulfilling, until you decrease or eliminate your **SIG** to a manageable capacity, and can laugh at yourself about it. The irony is you already know you are dominated by the responsibility of being powerful. You do not want to give in, because if you did, then you would have to do great stuff like your purpose and serving humanity in a super cool way, while being satisfied and fulfilled. As long as you continue to run those archaic **CD** programs, your life will not turn out optimally. You must design your way out. These eight steps do exactly that.

Now, I do not want to make lite of your issues or difficult circumstance. I am just making a point about the mechanism of what is at the root of the situation. While working with clients, I explore their stories very carefully with patience and compassion. We work together and use a number of strategies to untangle the meanings which are clogging up the great possibilities in their lives. We lessen, diminish and ultimately neutralize their perceived problems, stops and obstacles. This leaves them with freedom to express their creativity and imagination in the area of their optimal aptitude freely.

This is your opportunity for freedom. Ultimately this deepens your relationships at home and at work, forwarding all of your life and business goals. When you become willing to start practicing with the tools required to manage this in your life you will experience a sense of satisfaction and fulfillment at a high level. The quality of your life will continue to increase as long as you practice and apply yourself seriously to a level of mastery. You will be designing your life, a life by design, without being stopped by fear of the obstacles, which currently are holding you back. Some of your fears will disappear and some of them will continue. However, diminished, you will include them and move forward anyway, without consideration, because you have designed well and responsibly. You will become confident to jump off the edge of your choosing.

We are stronger together, our mass is larger, and our movement of sustainability for the planet is great. This is a purpose we all benefit from when we are aligned. We will focus on the specific areas of your life which are the most important to you, your family, your business, physical well-being and your spiritual connection.

We flourish while embracing unity and connectedness to our universal freedoms, focused on creativity and imagination and not our limitations and fears. Many cultural controls inhibit our ability to connect with the universal knowledge and wisdom available to us. Some of our cultural controls may have had good intentions initially, however like most old paradigms, they become archaic and are the next example of what does not work. Or worse, they continue to be embraced as if they are still relevant **(CD).** The problem with paradigms is they are always innovative when initially conceived and followed. However, as they age they become the next limiting factor (with few exceptions) in stifling our creativity and imagination towards generating the next paradigm. Realizing this distinction, opens up our ability to accessing higher consciousness, and our ultimate advantage in life. Our ability to design forward from here creates sustainability.

Ideas which become obsolete are the physical, social, cultural and spiritual barriers which separate us (**The Gap**) and keep us from the unity and connectedness we seek (resolute vs. a life by design, aka **CD** vs. **DCD**). Once domination, manipulation and control take hold in these entrenched paradigms any good that may have been present in them has now outlived its usefulness. Corruption is a clear sign that a paradigm is archaic and needs replacing. It has now become an example of how not to do things, it has become unsustainable and the opportunity becomes replacing it and to design it newly.

Governments, Religions, Corporations, Big Pharma, (with some exceptions) etc…who justify war, profits, weapons, drugs and foods which poison humanity while pushing chemotherapy, surgery, mandatory vaccines, addictive drugs for profits as an end to meet their survival may very well be the definition of criminally archaic. These entrenched anti-archetypes are the antithesis of the ills of our society today. With very few exceptions, do their benefits justify their means. Their conflict of interest is inherent in virtually everything they do (this is the default setting).

Many governments are made up of career politicians who have lost their way and stopped serving those who elected them, in favor of their own self-serving re-election campaigns. They intentionally block or prolong the implementation of solutions, by the over complication of relatively simple issues. Their conflict of interest between service and special interests, while protecting their overpaid jobs is corrupt. One set of rules for them and another for we the people. Perpetrating drug wars in the name of profits, while criminalizing the addiction of broken people is without thought. Excessive taxation which is over complicated, mean spirited and hateful in its structure and implementation, is not functional, sustainable or necessary. If it were about generating tax revenue there is a much more efficient and sustainable way. Many religions are made up of principles which separate us. It is a direct conflict and hypocritical to the type of work they proclaim to do. Corporations with exploitive practices and methods, generating billions of dollars annually, while producing products, goods and services that are poisoning the planet and dumbing down society at an alarmingly tragic and unsustainable rate, are another example of **CD.** Big Pharma is involved in creating customers and not cures. There is tremendous suffering that can be alleviated and healed which Big Pharma is fully aware of. Clients are what sustain them while fueling their profit machine. The health, wellbeing and a physically thriving public are not in their calculus. In few instances are they improving our lives more than the suffering they create.

Watch what people do, and not what they say. You have got to walk the walk, if you talk the talk. What is missing is sustainability and conscious capitalism, with compassion for humanity and our planet. Our ability to create new paradigms to replace these old archaic ones is our maximum contribution and expression of love for humanity and of our planet. All we have to do is start with ourselves and build this new foundation to launch from. A life by design allows for that future to be realized vs. the default setting which has brought us to this point in history, longing for sustainability and realizing our dreams. Start with yourself, your family and work, further increasing the circle to your community and humanity. Build your dream.

Enjoy the ride because you have a front row seat. This is not a practice life. Laugh, love, be passionate, take chances, be productive, learn something new every day, question everything in a curious open way, play, sweat, be fully self-expressed, be kind to one another, take naps, travel, eat different foods, cook, go surfing, play tennis, walk in nature, do yoga, go skiing, learn to dive and play in the oceans, dance, try all the sports you like and some you do not. Learning how to **Jump Off the Edge Responsibly**, it is your access to freedom and generating new paradigms. This is how we propel ourselves forward and increase the quality of life. We will not succeed by fixing the existing systems, which in large part are controlling and responsible for societies-ills. This is a less than optimal use of our energy and focus. Implementing what is missing in the way of sustainability and our connectedness is powerful and unifying. It is our collective alignment (speaking for and implementing new paradigms) and our best thinking which will have us forward sustainable programs for the humanity. We must redesign, implement a life by design, and build an improved sustainable way, while helping other across the bridge to our amazing future.

Life is experiential and without taking new risks our creativity can be diminished. It is the trial and error of life, the making of mistakes, that shows us how to design going forward. We are creating breakthroughs and mistakes over and over, in our spiraling trajectory, towards the direction of our newly created life. Making new mistakes is being creative and imaginative. Making the same mistakes over and over again is a decision until we choose otherwise.

Education is not something we can finish, it is our infinite adventure, the journey of our soul's evolution in the collective consciousness. It unites us in our pursuit to evolve and expand ourselves. It is our universal human condition, freedom and opportunity. Embracing these ideas allows us to create perspectives which accomplish anything our imagination can perceive. What could be more satisfying and enjoyable than that?

Time is a human construct in language which may have some useful applications. However, it does not exist as we think. Actually, all we have is now and now and now. Tomorrow never happens, there is no Free Beer Tomorrow! These precious few moments are all we have to be fully engaged. What we choose now and now and now are the gifts of our freedom to design exactly the lives we seek. We are capable of creating at an increasingly high level when our individual gifts, abilities and aptitudes are identified early in childhood. It is the opportunity of parents, our education system and society to nurture the advancement of these gifts as early on as they are detected. These new beings; our children, are innocent and not yet hardened or jaded by society. It is our responsibility to make sure they have a green light. To hinder their unique contribution to the world, which they were born to contribute to, is an action of our own demise. This is a great responsibility, an opportunity and perhaps our greatest resource for the advancement and longevity of our species participation in the universe. All lives matter! Leave no soul behind! We are one! This is our calling.

The important thing is not to stop questioning. *—Albert Einstein*

It is the constant questioning of our old paradigms, the challenging of ideas in a philosophical context, as well as a scientific one, that has us continue to manifest the transformation of our awakening on our upward spiraling journey. This is the challenge to generate the next perspective which forwards our development and communication as human beings in our collective awakening. As we generate new paradigms we ensure that stagnation and old entrenched ways of being will not remain pertinent past their usefulness. This my friend is **DCD.** Design forward.

Rust never sleeps. — Neil Young

We must take time to calm ourselves, to lay down and breathe deeply. While we reflect on our connectedness with the earth and humanity we may soften ourselves to service and a sense of compassion. We really have no problems, there is no right or wrong. Only what works and what does not work. We must release our judgement. What we have is an infinite amount of opportunities for a life by design, in the direction of our amazing dreams.

It is beneficial to begin addressing your top priorities early on in your inquiry so you start producing life changing results immediately. We will use as many different strategies as necessary to effectively breakthrough your **CD** as quickly as possible. You are going to love this. We are in an unpopular revolution which most of us do not discern. Never surrender your voice in your cause to help others understand **C**ognitive **D**issonance within themselves. Learning how to generate new distinctions and paradigms while leaving the old ones behind is freedom. Helping people use new tools has them generate new ways of thinking. This is our access to helping humanity across the bridge to a sustainable future, one in which we may all participate in for our mutual benefit and connection.

Time and space are not conditions in which we live, but modes by which we think. — *Albert Einstein*

Chapter 4 / Step Two
De Cognitive Dissonance
Creating New Perspectives

- **Step 2 De Cognitive Dissonance (DCD)**
Recognition of your power to create and
design. Differentiating your obstacles and
removing your stops. Generating new
interpretations which align with your
optimal aptitudes, talents and abilities to
propel you forward into your purpose and
maximum contribution to humanity, your
new life by design awaits. **Suffering Index
Gap (SIG)** is the time it takes to go from
CD to **DCD**.

The danger of our stories within **CD** is, we
mistake them for being true, and give them
meanings which they do not have, or are

inaccurate and mistaken. This is the trap you set for yourself. It is your challenge to identify these meanings you have attached to these stories which prevent you from having the life of your dreams. Understanding and creating distinctions lead you to the new paradigm. Integration of your creativity and imagination are the access to your freedoms and universal knowledge. If the world is your oyster then the universe is your pearl.

Focusing on the areas of your inspiration and passion is where you begin designing what is possible. A life more amazing than you could have dreamt is what awaits you.

Jumping off the edge in this instance is a passionate commitment to your own life. It is in the realization that no one can do it alone. Continuing to learn new ways or modalities is critical to that advancement. We really are connected beings, our consciousness is collective and when you are fully aligned (body, mind and soul), your ability to produce extraordinary results is maximized. Creating a life by design is about fully integrating all the components of your life in an optimal way for your unique gifts and aptitudes. This is where your ultimate satisfaction, fulfillment and joy reside.

Imagine being on vacation and meeting a guide, a Shaman, or healer, and really connecting. All of a sudden, your experience is enriched by this new relationship. You have a new friend. There is much to learn from your new friend and much to share with each other to forward your life experiences. These are the fruits of life which enrich us. To embrace these opportunities is the gift, and to miss them, is the moment you were not present to life. It was a gift you did not recognize. This is a universal human condition, and to become aware of it is the beginning of not missing a gift the next time. This is **DCD** in action.

Identifying the stories we have constructed in the most important areas of our lives (family, relationships, spirituality, work, health, satisfaction, fulfillment, trauma and our education, etc.) is an important step. Understanding the meaning you have attached to your stories, creating new plausible meanings or generating alternate interpretations which forward your action in the direction of your goal or purpose is freedom. The design advantage comes from becoming comfortable in the process. Realizing how easy it is to include or remove any old meaning or interpretation you assigned to your life, which did not work or serve your purpose. You do this by replacing it with a new perspective that works and is aligned with your purpose. Learning and practicing this with new insights and distinctions advances your ability of creating a life by design. This will give you the confidence and ability to continue generating additional perspectives. Your **SIG** is becoming very small now. This is your practice. Your default setting does not get to call the shots any longer.

Without accessing your ability to generate new perspectives and developing the necessary skills, your likelihood of accessing your potential creativity, imagination and freedom is restricted. Not learning this has hindered your dreams. You must become accountable and responsible for generating interpretations, meanings and perspectives which lead to new paradigms for yourself and your projects realization. This is how you create your exceptional life. This is your calling. It is your contribution and service to this means, which gives you deep satisfaction and fulfillment in your personal and business life. We need not be competitive or aggressive, but determined and open to helping others. The opportunity becomes improving your ability in connecting the dots and bringing the designed results to fruition. Another slant on this is setting your conviction free. Let go of what is not working for you. Keep designing forward.

Taking the practical steps required to make it occur, requires your commitment and focus in making the results you want real. With an investment in yourself, a strong commitment and the proper focus you will begin to generate insights and results that you were not able to create before. You begin to have an experience of excitement and satisfaction. A new sense of confidence begins to emerge as you learn to apply these new tools in your life. You perceive yourself into existence. As you continue to define your guiding perspectives, so you design your life.

So, humanities' opportunity becomes De Cognitive Dissonance (**DCD**). It is your integration of creativity and your construction of alternative perspectives which gives you access to designing the life you hunger for. It is critical to acknowledge the existence of Cognitive Dissonance (**CD**) in the world and our ability to identify it in the areas where we find ourselves without opportunities for action. Equally important is the Suffering

Index Gap (**SIG**) and increasing your ability to minimize the time it takes you to go from **CD** to **DCD**. It is in making these types of distinctions which allows you the power to implement effective change in a meaningful and contributory way. Otherwise, it is virtually impossible to break out of the old patterns which your Cognitive Dissonance restricts or limits you. **CD** is where all of your stops and obstacles reside.

It will be the ability of your continued learning and adaptation towards the development of your cognitive agility, which will have you flourish in society. All the while integrating these skills into changing your perceptions at will. **DCD** is a key component and design tool for the Quantum Universe in which we are now living.

De Constructing Cognitive Dissonance!
One Paradigm at A Time

Imagination is more important than knowledge. Knowledge is limited. Imagination encircles the world. — *Albert Einstein*

Chapter 5 / Step Three
Cognitive Agility
Standing on Solid Ground

- **Step 3 Cognitive Agility (CA):** Practicing CD, DCD and SIG distinctions.

Getting your hands on the wheel and beginning to generate your own insights, distinctions and paradigms. Your creativity, imagination and confidence is increasing.

This is where a life by design starts to take off!

Be mindful that to connect with the collective consciousness or hear your constructive inner voice, you need to keep clearing up the **CD** conversation in your mind. By paying attention to your considerations and concerns, they can be addressed and diminished. It is in the addressing and completing those incompletions which frees you up to replace those distractions with something contributory. To the degree you free yourself from these old thoughts and paradigms, is the degree to which you are free to create that which you are inspired by most. Remember that those hindering conversations are held in place by meanings that are untrue or no longer accurate. You may do this by playfully generating new interpretations using metaphors. An example of this is a bridge to your future. This forward's your designed life in the direction of your practical plan, using your key aptitudes and skill sets. This will help visualize specifically for you, your family, project, business, community, or any organizational goals. Leaving CD behind while being on the DCD bridge to your CA future. The natural progression of this path is increased synchronicity, and your integrated alignment with your purpose.

Practicing **CD** and **DCD** distinctions expands your cognitive agility (**CA**). Your conviction and ability to change perception holds the key to solution generation, problem solving and implementation. As you become more comfortable in your practice you will increase your connection and awareness to our universal knowledge. This is something you begin the feel at the level of your soul, this is real and a function of how much self, love you develop; being your own best friend. As with all life, this is a process and not an event. It requires focus, commitment and setting life priorities. How bad do you really want it?

The pen is mightier than the sword. The word processor is mightier than the pen. Word press is mightier than the word processor. Virtual reality is mightier than word press. Artificial intelligence (AI) is mightier than virtual reality. The Quantum Universe is mightier than AI. Consciousness is mightier that the Quantum Universe. As far as we can tell nothing is mightier than Consciousness. It does however beg the question, what is behind Consciousness? We are one.

When you restrain your potential, for any number of reasons, (such as, reasonableness) you prematurely limit your imagination and creativity, which is your source to achieving the life of your dreams. Jumping off the edge of reasonableness (a form of **CD**) into the **DCD** and questioning everything newly facilitates your amazing life. You develop a new perspective which forwards the motion and takes action. Your sense of urgency will pull results to you like a magnet. Hesitancy is your Cognitive Dissonance (**CD**) raising its ugly head and prolonging your Suffering Index Gap (**SIG**).

By generating new perspectives with playful urgency and gifting yourself with increased awareness of our universal knowledge, you expedite your mastery of Cognitive Agility (**CA**). It is the realization of our oneness which awakens us as we become more aligned. We are here to help others so we may grow together. We are the bridge to a higher calling, assisting others to access their optimal aptitudes and purpose so their creativity and imagination will be free to generate the most positive contribution they are capable of making. This cycle increases the quality of life for everyone, even if they are not yet participating actively. By instilling this reasoning in your family, relationships or corporate responsibilities makes an amazing difference in the quality of what you are building.

One of your keys here is remaining focused. You are awake now. Your sense of service is heightened and your heart filled with gratitude. You are a Cognitive Agility Ninja in action. Increasing your level of mastery in this area works to increase your access to deeper resources, with all the tools.

Jumping off the edge is a metaphor for your Cognitive Agility (**CA**) and your actual ability to adapt and change often and rapidly in any situation. It is about using your practical tools which allow you to generate new perspectives and results. This brings you to a safe landing place until another opportunity to jump off the edge presents itself. After developing a degree of skill and confidence, by increasing your cognitive agility, you ultimately develop your own unique awareness to generate and create new distinctions which become the primary tools for paradigm shifting. Increasing your level of mastery in jumping off the edge allows you greater access to information in the collective. It helps to solidify your understanding and the implementation of your projects goals and purpose.

As you think, so shall you become.
—Bruce Lee

Chapter 6 / Step Four
Mindfulness / Body Mind Soul
It is not so unless you say it is
Being your Best Friend

- **Step 4 Integrating Your Practice** into your body, mind and soul. It is all about optimizing your system and becoming your best friend, while increasing your- self value and self-love. This is where managing your well-being becomes your priority so you are nurtured and have the ability for maximum contribution. Being healthy, balanced and present allows for flow to happen.

Examples of areas to practice mastery of Cognitive Agility (CA)

1. Your relationships, personal and business.

2. How you interact in the world sustainably.

3. Your stress triggers, anxiety and emotions.

4. Diet, exercise, sleep and your internal conversation.

5. Your spiritual connection.

A physically challenging practice that exercises your body is imperative to access your optimal potential. For me it is surfing, swimming, skiing and yoga. I highly recommend yoga for everyone in every state of health. The point is doing something consistently to increase your balance between body, mind and soul for your overall well-being integration. What do you enjoy that will become your daily practice? Creating balance and flow with life integrates our masculine and feminine at the level of the soul. Including as well, all beings and matter. We are one, the universal equation knows not superiority, discrimination, prejudice or bigotry. The color of our skin, our sexual preferences, spiritual beliefs or gender have nothing to do with us as spiritual beings, having a human experience. We have lessons and opportunities for learning and bridging gaps on our infinite trajectory to optimize our contribution for humanity. When we distinguish a new gap we have an opportunity, a real purpose to design what's missing, and to fill in the gap. Sometimes the gap is information, knowledge, emotions or feelings. Maybe it is social, cultural, spiritual or simply taking a specific step or action which has the last dots be connected in your beautifully designed life. When your life is fully integrated your freedom is maximized.

Yoga may be intimidating for some however, it need not be. There is no need to have your practice in public unless you are comfortable doing so. There are many ways to practice in the privacy of your own home.

Start with reading some books or watching some videos, you will learn what serves you. The point is to participate for yourself, to pay attention to your breath, listen to your body and quiet your mind. Yoga can be very meditative as well, just dive in and play with it. Soon enough you will find your balance and some grounding; a connection to the collective consciousness which comes with it. If you desire or when you become ready there are many public classes and instructors who will love to help you deepen your practice.

I have found that creating a consistent routine facilitates managing my well being physically, emotionally and spiritually. I have been practicing yoga for over 30 years and about 7 years ago I invested in myself and completed a teacher training program to deepen my practice, not with the intention of becoming a yoga instructor. I was receiving so much value from my practice that I wanted to deepen it, by jumping off the edge and committing to more training and insights.

One of the things I enjoy about my practice is the peace that comes with it. The overall mindfulness and ability to integrate body, mind and soul optimally is satisfying and soothing to my wellbeing. A daily ritual enhances your ability to focus and prioritize your wellbeing. For me, it begins early each morning before 5:00 AM, waking with the Howler monkeys. It is dark and otherwise quiet and still. I am appreciative for this beautiful beginning, making our coffee, having fresh juice with Kathryn's nutritious homemade cookies and moringa, ginger and turmeric homemade supplements. The quiet time is great for meditation and reflection for the day ahead. On the floor in shavasana, (a yoga-pose, laying on my back, arms at my sides and palms facing down for grounding) I check in with myself. My life by design revolves around managing my wellbeing. When my integration is optimal, (meaning I have balance within my body, mind and soul) the quality of my contribution is powerful and in direct correlation with my connection to others and my elevated internal conversation. Making time for meditation in an integrated life is a huge gift we give to ourselves. I am very grateful for my practice and what it continues to open up for me. I am spending 20-40 minutes on the floor every morning, depending on how I feel. Less if I am good to go and longer if I need to check my modality and body further. I will often return to the floor to stretch throughout the day as I feel the need. Few things could be more-simple to connect and focus me. Now it is time for hygiene and more coffee, selecting the proper surfboard for the days conditions, checking equipment, leash, fins tight, combing and wax the board and loading the car. Mango is in the back of the car on his bed and Kathryn is my copilot. Her beach bag is filled with water, a thermos, her famous cookies, painting supplies to capture the magnificent waves she paints and her homemade bug repellent and sunscreen. We are prepared for a morning at the beach.

It is now approximately 6:30 AM. We are on our way to surfing, depending on all the variables and conditions, wind, tides, swell size and direction, time of year, crowd control, driving time, etc…and I am catching my first wave between 6:45 and 7:15. While I am waiting on my sets, I meditate. I have time to receive all the insights my muse, the ocean, has to offer that day. My relationship with the ocean is a deep connection which feeds my energy to create and be imaginative, some of my best insights occur while I am surfing. I belong, I am home and at peace. Everyone has something or some place that will create this type of clarity and focus for them. I love hearing my clients describe theirs.

Normally, I will surf 2 hours then return home to shower and I will be at my computer by 9:30 forwarding my projects. I am speaking with my first client at 10:00 am. Kathryn whips up a fresh fruit smoothie of frozen banana, papaya and pineapple blended with fresh ginger juice and flor de Jamaica (hibiscus) tea for us. Productivity is about efficiency and focus and not being busy. Busy is a story we tell ourselves to rationalize or justify something usually tied to procrastination, part of the **CD** which I am monitoring every moment. Cognitive Dissonance (**CD**) is the thief of our greatness and causes us unnecessary stress, drama and suffering.

I am a bit of a grazer. I work best eating small healthy snacks throughout the day. I enjoy celery and carrot sticks with a handful of almonds at my desk for energy. Lunch and nap time are optional, depending on what needs accomplishing that day. However, naps are strongly advised and a great time for afternoon delight; creating space and intimacy with your partner. We all have our own rhythm and you need to find yours. Nurturing and touching each other and taking care of each other is natural. Sexual generosity generates a greater intimacy and connection between you and your partner. The exchange of energy is a gift we share with each other. Enjoy your bodies and play. Linger, breathe, connect and appreciate the physicality of life.

It is a digital world you can accomplish and create virtually anything from anywhere. I complete any unfinished details, coaching calls, or daily goals and prepare for the following day. Normally, I will prioritize the top three items and make sure they are complete before moving on to other priorities. It is critical to remain focused on your primary goal, make time for your one thing. Mine is coaching and to create sustainability in people's lives and for the planet. I am assisting individuals, groups and organizations to forward their creation of a life by design which fits their specific goals.

Around 5:00 pm, it's time for another trip to the beach to check the waves. If they are good I surf, if not, we take Mango for a walk on the beach and enjoy the sunset together. We always prepare a delicious and nutritious dinner. It is our time together, nurturing our relationship as a couple with our phones put away. After dinner is the time to check any communication that requires urgency and respond. Otherwise, it can wait until tomorrow. Sleep is critical. I like to get 7-8 hours. That being said, it is about balance and mindfulness, so you will adjust accordingly. We can all push forward on a lot less sleep, but it is not sustainable for the long haul. It is proven that 6 hours or less is not enough to sustain your overall well-being and operate optimally. Eventually, lack of sleep will create deficiencies, stress and even lead to burn out in your career. If you are an active thinker and sometimes get less than optimal sleep, get up, do not resist it. You can nap later. Make some herbal tea and grab a note pad and write it out. This is when some of your clarity will come out as insights, which will become the basis for the new distinctions you will create. This is magic time, so embrace it and include it. This is part of your gift, so please indulge yourself. You will now be able to go back to bed and sleep. You will be surprised at what comes to you when you are open to this. Begin taking action immediately on any of these insights as soon as you can, when they are still fresh and your excitement is high.

Remember, a schedule is good. Simple is better and less is more, abundance gives you unlimited options to implement the exact life by design you are creating for yourself. Go now! Do not hesitate. This is your life. Create a sense of playful and calm urgency while managing your core wellbeing. We are one and you are not alone. This is your grounding space, grounding yourself (Body, Mind and Soul), being active, eating nutritiously, gifting yourself with universal connectedness. Enjoying peace, love and compassion while making your optimal contribution is your purpose. You only need to define your life by design specifics for your unique aptitude and abilities to align with your contribution. Consistent behavior creates consistent outcomes. Continue moving in the direction of your goals. You are an unstoppable force of nature. As always, the best is yet to come. A life by design is a creative process with much more happiness, joy, satisfaction and fulfillment than a non-designed life. Your default setting will run you, if you do not run it. Your life really is in your hands so choose well and generate greatness!

I wanted to share some simple things which make a big difference in my practice: **Simple is better and less is more.**

- Call someone when you are missing them

- Invite someone when you want to see them

- Explain something when you want to be understood

- Ask when you have a question

- Say with grace when you do not like something

- Tell someone when you do like something

- Ask for it when you want something

- Tell people you love them when you do

A life which works is a series of habits which work that you practice.

- Get plenty of rest

- Brush your teeth often

- Make your bed

- Get on the floor to stretch out and meditate

- Go surfing or walk on the beach

- Do your laundry and clean house

- Have your favorite coffee or tea

- Wash your dishes as you go

- Take your vitamins, garden or grow food and flowers

- Make art; do something creative

- Get on the floor and do your practice; stretch your body

- Make quiet time for planning your designed life

- Mindful nutrition and balance; eat what you love and be healthy

- Communicate effectively and be on time

- Take naps, hug, kiss and love yourself

- Love your life and others, be generous and have gratitude

- Work productively while choosing well and loving what you do

- Exercise, play, walk, go dancing and laugh a lot!

- Help someone without them knowing

- Learn something new every day and be creative and imaginative

- Wear your seat belt or a helmet always

- Have a budget and spend your money supporting sustainability

- Be kind to one another and show appreciation

- Eat birthday cake and pop balloons

- Be your own best friend and elevate your internal conversation

- Sleep well, live well and anything else you can add; do it well

All those things we worry about, along with the questions and planning to resolve situations are not what 'gets' us. What 'gets' us, is the thing we never considered and never saw coming. If you can conceive it, then there is a solution. Do not spend your time over thinking. That is a source of suffering you don't have to have in your life.

Things do not change we change —
Thoreau

Chapter 7 / Step Five
Paradigms and Distinctions
Becoming Comfortable /
Changing them Quickly

Find your style of life and keep fine tuning it, practice according to your own conditions and perspectives, while aligning your Cognitive Agility. — Finny

- **Step 5 Defining Your Purpose** By using the tools from your practice this far, we explore your passions and dreams further. We are able to forward an optimal life by design strategy and have a practical look over the edge! We consider the logistical issues and prepare for a beautiful landing.

Understand Paradigm, Distinction and Insight:

A paradigm, in science, philosophy and any other area for that matter, is a distinct set of concepts or thought patterns, including theories, research methods, postulates, and standards for what constitutes legitimate contributions to a field or any area of thought.

A distinction is a contrast between similar things or people, the separation of things into different groups according to their attributes or characteristics and something that sets someone or something apart from others. A means of comparison by division to illustrate a point.

An insight is an understanding of a specific cause and effect in a specific context. It is the content inside of one of your life domains. Often times these are the connecting the dots ideas which come to us throughout our lives. The good news is when we take time to integrate them into our life by design their value becomes very important in the ultimate construct of what it is that we are building. The bad news is most people do not take the time to do the integration and connect the dots in a meaningful and powerful way which adds value to their life. This is the equivalent of reading the book without practicing the concepts.

It is important to journal and take notes as you have those ideas before they get away. This is another great habit to reinforce, so write often. You will find it useful to start transferring these notes to your lap top or tablet, so that your source material will be in one place. When you are ready, start defining your optimal plan for action in the area of your purpose. When you begin to put this in writing your creativity and imagination will show you a new gear you did not know you had. This is one reason your integration and balance are so important. You need to be clear and focused to perform optimally.

These are powerful words; **paradigm**, **distinction**, and **insight.** They are tools to exercise your creativity, imagination and self-expression. They include all the areas of humanity; our language, art, science, spirituality and our physicality, for starters. We can begin to model anything we can imagine and literally the sky is the limit living in this quantum universe with the approaching Artificial Intelligence (AI) singularity. The point at which AI will exceed or over take human intelligence is the AI Singularity. Yes, amazing times indeed, with many new questions. As information continues to accelerate, surpassing our human ability to digest it, it is increasingly important to incorporate The Eight Steps of life by design into your unique life. It is in the realization of your optimal aptitudes and abilities and designing your life into the area of your purpose and optimal contribution, which will have you experience greater satisfaction and fulfillment. You can connect deeply with the source and access a higher purpose by remembering what it is you forgot, and by learning what it is you do not know, then accessing what it is you do not know that you do not know. Now that's something to think about, huh? Stay curious my friends and keep designing forward your beautiful vision.

There is something about models, paradigms, distinctions and insights, that are ultimately mistaken (with few exceptions).

Yet, most of us do not relate to them in this way. They are only the best level of thinking we have evolved to currently. It is optimal to hold them as such. They are good ideas to build on until superior creativity takes hold, giving rise to our next layer or level of advancement. This is the process of our universal **DCD** and the source of all issues which separate us, making us unique, yet unifying us, because we are not resolute about them being true. It is this inclusion and your ability to change quickly and adapt efficiently that has us be united. You must be open to give up being right about anything. Recognizing this and embracing **DCD** by using your creativity and imagination, in the area of your optimal aptitude, has you be accountable and responsible for generating an interpretation that forwards the action of your purpose, project, goals and optimal contribution, in an altruistic way for your desired results. Practicing this, your Cognitive Agility (**CA**) increases as you experience this happening in your life in real time now. You must realize there is no right or wrong, only what works and what does not work (removing judgement). Unraveling the meaning of life is a moving target and one which has significant consequences when you do not recognize this point. Life has no correct answer. It is a paradox you manage creatively and with your unique style. The right or wrong paradigm is a major source of suffering. If I were to enroll the world into disallowing a paradigm; this is the one!

Everything is resolvable inside of communication and specifically inside of promises and requests. As you design solutions and implement them they are certain to become the next example of what we will eventually improve upon. So, it is your ability to change quickly and to implement the next insight which becomes the new distinction, that is your next grounding paradigm, until it is not. The cycle of the process is beautiful and one we will benefit from as more people participate in this process. Imagine a world where everyone was practicing the 8 steps of life by design. A world where our division and fear based beliefs were archaic ideas from the past. We are living in unity, as one connected universally with each other, living in our collective consciousness. We are living a life by design. This is not far-fetched. It is within our realization in this generation, when we say so.

Imagine all the people   *— John Lennon*

Becoming your own best friend is a great endeavor and one which allows you to become the best version of yourself. We all have needs, rituals, a sense of adventure, and the desire to be appreciated. We hunger for loving connections between friends and our partner. You will continue to learn and grow and to educate yourself in the direction of your inspiration and abilities. It is all within your ability to understand this and execute a life by design. Including these things, along with being prosperous and satisfied, simplifies being your own best friend. It is primarily your internal conversation which is the barometer for how you are doing in this regard. Be kind with yourself, take it easy and remember you are precious and valuable. This is what is critical to the integration of your authentic self. This is your universal gift, if you allow yourself to have it. If you do not give yourself permission to, then who will? As previously solved, you truly get to choose your own interpretation. Do you choose suffering or greatness, unfortunately or fortunately? Choose now in your present moment. This is **DCD** in action.

You either default to **CD** (suffering and/or unfortunately) or move on to a **DCD** (greatness and/or fortunately) interpretation, because you say so. This is your Cognitive Agility (**CA**), reducing your Suffering Index Gap (**SIG**) and further reinforcing the 'if you do not give yourself permission to, then who will' conversation. Creating a life by design is a gift you give yourself, when your conviction is high and you are integrating the tools into the components of your designed life, flow happens naturally. You are grounded and confident.

Cognitive Dissonance / Elevate it
De Cognitive Dissonance / Reframe it
Cognitive Agility / Metaphor it

The faster you are able to change the better. It is your ability to adapt by using your unrestricted creativity and imagination to perceive new interpretations, insights, distinctions and paradigms. Fill any remaining resentments with gratitude and appreciation so you may be present now to your present. It is simply reframing any negative interpretation or experience with a creative and imaginative one. One which generates greatness out of that moment, so, you are left inspired with energy to re-engage powerfully and constructively.

In our lifetimes, it seems as if half of what we were told is not true and often what we were told which was true, is no longer completely accurate. This is the disconnect you are living into, and without being aware of it and having the tools, strategies, knowledge and inclination, you are lost. You are living in a fantasy world based on lies, half-truths and archaic paradigms. This is change in action at your door step. This is what you are adapting into. To miss this point, or to not have an awareness of the nature and effect of this type of natural change, limits your progress as if you were riding a tricycle while racing a Tesla.

As you continue to increase your **CA**, along with your integrated body, mind and soul, your balance, clarity and attention to detail are improving. Your ability to create contemporary distinctions from your insights and generating new paradigms has taken hold in your life. You are connecting the dots in a powerful way now and defining your focus and purpose. Your awareness of and connection to the quality of your relationships is strengthening and pulling you into your freedom and to the contribution you are here to make to your family and work projects, while creating your dream life. You are experiencing a sense of calmness and serenity in your oneness. You are home. Breathe in gratitude and exhale love with your internal relationship and those in your life.

There is no path to peace; peace is the path.
—Gandhi

Chapter 8 / Step Six
We are the bridge to the future
We design
Dimensional Awareness

- Step 6 The Dimensional Bridge:

Recognition of where you are on the bridge allows for fine tuning your life by design and making adjustments, while being accountable, responsible and anticipating the unknown. You are fully aware of your purpose, your connection with the collective consciousness and the importance of your contribution to humanity.

Let's consider your dimensional awareness and use the metaphor of a bridge. We will connect your natural progression along that path physically, socially, culturally and spiritually as you are expanding your abilities to deepen your unity and connectedness. You have a vast number of paradigms to construct along this path as you replace the old ones. These new paradigms represent your expanded knowledge, understanding and wisdom as you remember, awaken to, and become aware of your purpose.

Synchronicity is our beautiful universe aligned!

We are dimensional beings. In fact, we are multi-dimensional being's way beyond our current comprehension. As our earthly consciousness awakens to its higher dimensional awareness, a clear example emerges to illustrate some of these paradigms, and/or the generation of these distinctions. This is the dimensional bridge. Our states of consciousness influence our perceptions of life, likewise, our perceptions also influence our states of consciousness. It seems to be that nothing trumps consciousness, although it is an interesting question to think about. Life is a multidimensional paradoxical highway, with many adventures. Continue exploring your optimal aptitudes and abilities, while using your strongest skills. This allows deeper access to your creativity and imagination, which gives you real freedom for the expression of your purpose in the form of your contribution to humanity. Your deep connection to the collective allows you greater insights to the knowledge and wisdom of our universal possibilities. All of this translates into you being the best you. Manifesting your dreams through the practical implementation of creating your life by design.

Metaphors are a great tool in the combined visualization and articulation of our ability to model new thinking, distinctions or paradigms.

I think it is important for you to understand the three models I describe as:

3D consciousness, **4D** consciousness and **5D** consciousness.

3D consciousness is an archaic **CD** model. The universe shows up as a volume and life as we experience it is now possible. This is when it starts to get interesting. Let's begin in a Newtonian Universe, where we perceive from a physical state. We see ourselves as individuals and separate beings not connected. Darwinian (survival of the fittest), being aggressive and in a competitively driven world where the car you drive, the job you have, the money you make and your surroundings define you. You define things as good or bad, right or wrong. You have a sense of scarcity with happiness and fulfillment which are defined by your bank account and social status. Our thoughts have minimal impact on reality and life is one coincidence after another. We find joy in living with our five senses, however generating deeper meaning and understanding are a struggle. We are just beginning to learn how to generate distinctions which will propel us forward to new thinking, new perspectives and paradigms.

4D / 20thC Consciousness is a transitional, awakening, **DCD** model. We become more aware of our connectedness and life has an optimistic possibility about it. The unknown is enticing and our creativity and imagination are increasing. This is referred to as the

Einsteinian Universe. We begin generating distinctions which change the way we experience reality. We may still be living in a right or wrong world however, our questioning of these perspectives is increasing. We have become mindful of our well-being, health, nutrition and connectedness to the planet. We are driven to grow, learn and pursue our purpose. Connecting the dots is increasingly exciting. We are further improving our ability to generate meaningful distinctions which help to design a life we love. Our innate intuition begins to emerge furthering our ability to perceive and expand what is possible for us as a connected species. However, we are experiencing global crisis in many regards. The least of which is we are still primarily a hydrocarbon based society, with rampant corruption, poverty, and disease. Where Fukushima type disasters are going virtually unreported. Basically, an overall lack of global leadership in regard to crossing the **4D** / 20thC bridge to reach our **5D** / 21stC future. One of my primary purposes is to forward this learning, awareness and connectedness. In making this a public conversation where everyone benefits in all areas.

These old sources of power are being replaced to the degree we are aligned and connected while implementing solutions for our global sustainability.

5D / 21stC Consciousness is an awakening, new paradigms, **CA** model. Our senses are sharpened and our ability to go back to archaic ways of thinking are still possible, however, doing so may generate a sense of suffering (**CD),** since these 3D and 4D ways of being no longer work for us or ring accurate. We have understood first hand, the flaws and injustice from 3D and 4D modalities. We are now beginning to understand our unity in the Quantum Universe. We understand the connectedness of all beings and matter and we are experiencing a sense of joy and peace. We have replaced right and wrong with being accountable and responsible for generating interpretations that work too forward the motion for any outcome we are building towards. Discrimination and judgement are replaced by love, compassion, gratitude, acceptance and unity. People are unique yet connected and are equally experiencing happiness and joy in the areas of their optimal aptitudes and contributions. We are living in a time of decreasing war and violence. We are aligned in our physical, social, cultural and spiritual sustainability for the planet. Clean energies now dominate the earth.

The duality of life still remains. However, we have it and it does not have us. Our challenge, purpose and privilege is to connect with those who have not yet connected the dots or understood the possibilities of the 5D paradigm. As we develop our mastery here, the results of all our projects really are a matter of implementation and finalizing details for completion. You are a **CA** Ninja. We are sharing our experience, life insights, love and joy. The 4D is the bridge to our 5D future, until it is not and then the 5D will become the bridge to our 6D future. We are ever mindful of the gap we are living into, and our ability to design forward, optimally into an improved outcome or result. This is freedom!

Great minds discuss ideas, average minds discuss events, small minds discuss people.
— *Eleanor Roosevelt*

Eleanor brings up a good point. I started to think about some modalities that we use in language when we are discussing ideas, events and people. What comes up is speaking **about** ideas, events and people and speaking **for** ideas, events and people.

Speaking: "The action of conveying information or expressing one's thoughts and feelings in spoken language"

Speaking about: On the subject of concerning, so as to affect, to indicate movement within a particular area, used to express location in a particular place, used to describe a quality apparent in a person. This is where gossip lives, judgement, criticism, angst, suffering, regret, not being present, reactionary behavior, the drama zone and fear this is where 3D resides. This is also where the suffering index gap (**SIG**) is maximized and your **CD** is calling the shots. It has you, you do not have it. Anxiety is a practice and not a problem, you are easily aggravated. The question is what are you committed to and what is your conviction?

Speaking for: In support of or in favor of an idea, event, policy or person. Affecting with regard to, or in respect of an idea, event, policy or person. On behalf of or to the benefit of, as a purpose or function, as a reason or cause, as a destination, in place of or in exchange for, in relation to the expected norm of. It is generative, constructive and forwarding the motion of an idea, event, policy or person. This is where observation without judgement lives, creativity, generative process, gratitude, being present, being focused, your freedom and greatness. This is where 5D / 21stC resides. This is where the **SIG** is minimized or non-existent and your **CA** is powerful. You have it, it does not have you! This is your practice and your opportunity to increase the level of mastery in your designed life. Your mindful practice, optimal creativity, imagination and contribution to humanity are inspiring. Being in alignment in this way has your efficiency in life be maximized. The results you have been designing and building towards live here because you say so. **You have given yourself a green light, you are unstoppable.**

If we have no peace it is because we have forgotten we belong to each other. —
Mother Teresa

Chapter 9 / Step Seven
Looking over the Edge
The Pause Principle / Mastery of Mindfulness

- Step 7 The Pause Principle / Mastery of Mindfulness: You are on the bridge grounded and including your fears with confidence. Standing on the edge you are **Jumping Off the Edge Responsibly** into your gift.

Designing your specific plan with a focused outcome requires organization and a practical plan to implement. You may do it on your own at your pace or request assistance to accelerate your results. Your unique situation and stage in life play a significant role in your optimal life by design structure. It is not one size fits all. I will help you define your specific aptitudes, abilities and passions while we identify your purpose for your newly designed life. This experience is satisfying and fulfilling. Designing your dream life is incredible. Any emptiness you were experiencing will dissipate and eventually disappear as you continue your practice and as your level of mastery increases. You will be experiencing life as you have never experienced it before. You will have a new-found energy and excitement. You will continue accessing new insights and information which previously you did not have access to. Old patterns and stops will no longer have the power over you they once did. You are now free from that limiting **CD** thinking. It is important to look over the edge and assess the landing before taking your jump. Jumping Off the Edge Responsibly is amazing because you are including any remaining fear you have and doing it anyway simply because you say so. You are accountable and responsible for generating your own experiences. You are confident in a new way you have not known before. Your ability to generate this at will, across all the domains of your life are within your reach. It is only a matter of creating a life by design. Here is to your amazing landing!

The Pause Principle / Mastery of Mindfulness

Continuing to connect the dots.

1.) Your brain is a natural bridge to others, to our collective consciousness, connecting us and making us one.

2.) The point of communication is to decrease suffering and increase freedom. Increasing your clarity and patience are vital. Mindfulness leads you to mutual respect understanding and progress in the conversation, always forwarding the motion of your trajectory.

3.) Mindfulness practice takes concentration and focus. It is what you do to be aligned, if you are to be present to the gifts of life.

4.) As you continue your practice of mastery, you are constantly expanding your **CA** and adjusting your design to fit your purpose and contribution.

> *Our prime purpose in this life is to help others.* — *Dali Lama*

A bridge is worth a thousand words. Enjoy being on the bridge. This is what there is to do. While looking over the edge you are assessing where you are, while being mindful of where you are going, and what you are building. **This is our movement our opportunity for sustainability of the planet and humanity. It is my purpose and privilege to help as many people as possible to cross this bridge.** As I write this, I am jumping off the edge responsibly to create more sustainable ways to live and towards a less hydrocarbon dependent society. Physical sustainability (cleaner energy, organic foods, less pollution, and cleaning up the mess from our old paradigms), Social sustainability (crossing the 4D bridge), Cultural sustainability (global implementation of social sustainability), and Spiritual sustainability (we are spiritual beings having a human experience, we are one). My inspiration comes from helping others to define what they excel in and then assisting them in designing their way forward to a goal which aligns with their purpose. I am looking forward to assisting you with yours. **You are ready to Jump Off the Edge Responsibly.**

Darkness cannot drive out darkness;
only light can do that.
Hate cannot drive out hate;
only love can do that.
-Martin Luther King

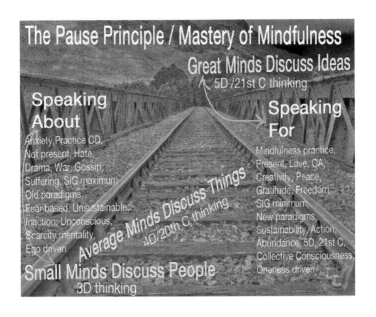

The Pause Principle / Mastery of Mindfulness

Great Minds Discuss Ideas

5D /21st C thinking

Speaking About

Anxiety, Practice CD, Not present, Hate, Drama, War, Gossip, Suffering, SIG maximum, Old paradigms, Fear based. Unsustainable. Inaction, Unconscious, Scarcity mentality, Ego driven

Speaking For

Mindfulness practice, Present, Love, CA, Creativity, Peace, Gratitude, Freedom, SIG minimum, New paradigms, Sustainability, Action, Abundance, 5D, 21st C, Collective Consciousness, Oneness driven

Average Minds Discuss Things

4D/20th C thinking

Small Minds Discuss People

3D thinking

The Pause Principle / Mastery of Mindfulness is a tool to locate yourself on the bridge. It is very useful in knowing where you are. Finding yourself on the bridge allows you to align with what it is you are designing to create. Our imagination and creativity are optimal in 5D (upper right). Models are always valuable as long as they are relevant, and currently this model is very relevant. It represents our awakening and our ability to improve our connection with the collective consciousness while creating a sustainable future for humanity and the planet. This image will allow you to orient yourself if you are pulled back by your **CD** into 3D (lower left) ways. Forever being mindful of your **SIG** and your innate ability to re-focus to the present is key to continue crossing the 4D Bridge to the 5D future. Life is to be enjoyed and experienced yet, sometimes we witness suffering. We can recognize it is a good teacher when we encounter it. Stay present and keep a light heart, one based on compassion, generosity and love. Jump now! Keep designing forward, your amazing life!

Ignorance is the greatest evil in the world. The friction which results from ignorance, and which is greatly increased owing to the number of languages and nationalities, can be reduced only by the spread of knowledge and the unification of the heterogeneous elements of humanity. No effort could be better spent. Our Ultimate Purpose — Buddha

Chapter 10 / Step Eight
Jumping Off the Edge
Responsibly into Your Gift
You Are an Unstoppable Force of
Nature

- **Step 8 Elevate Your Practice of Mastery:**
  Continuing your integration while
  increasing your awareness and ability to
  access the synchronicity and execute on
  your purpose. Sharing with others your
  growth and practice, being of service, and
  preparing to jump off the next edge.

We are spiritual beings, having a human
experience while forwarding our balance into
the universe. We have an Innate
connectedness to the collective consciousness;
the synchronicity. To the degree we are able
to exercise our Cognitive Agility is the degree

to which our maximum contribution will manifest and connect with who we are. Being aligned and having an integrated life with balance of body, mind and soul are a gift you give to yourself. Proceed with confidence, this is your inquiry into your journey, including issued hardware and software components. You are capable of abilities you are not yet aware of. It is the intention of this book to inform you on key elements which will lead to the optimization of your abilities while focusing on your strongest aptitudes and skill sets.

You were issued the following:

- A Body (your protective casing and hardware)

- Some DNA (chromosomes and software running most of your programs)

- Brain (a chip linked to our collective consciousness)

- Your Consciousness (a portal to our universal knowledge, wisdom and connectedness)

Let's consider the possibility of there being one mind and all consciousness is connected multidimensional in an expanding Quantum Universe, including all beings and matter as we know it. You are pure energy. Also consider the possibility

179

that the manifestation of the evolution of your consciousness to infinity is what you are capable of. Ram Dass – Reframe. This leaves a lot of room for creativity, imagination and the implementation of anything you are committed to designing in your relationships, family and business projects. How great can you stand to have your life be?

Going from CD to DCD in one second!

You are a soul connected to the collective consciousness, you have a body not the other way around. To miss this point is critical to the optimal performance in your life. You are a spiritual being having a human experience. You have had many experiences and will have many more. Lessons are repeated until they are learned, generating new distinctions and perspectives which accomplish the task of having learned the lesson. An increase in the level of your challenge will occur as you continue to learn and remember more advanced lessons. Initially, learning occurs linearly until your non-linear learning skills emerge allowing access to a deeper utilization of your new perspectives and applying them powerfully. This is termed transformational learning. Old cultural paradigms and reasonableness are not obstacles which impede your progress any longer. You are always witnessing gaps in your knowledge and understanding. This is your opportunity to put in what's missing in a creative and imaginative way. Enjoy the process moment by moment, as if it were a dance or some art form expressing your creation of a life by design.

Initially, simple is better and after having gone through your inventory process while categorizing, compartmentalizing and editing your life there is an amazing relief; a de stressing that occurs. Identifying, prioritizing and implementing the practical aspects in alignment with your desired results, makes your new life by design real. Taking the high road 4D bridge to your 5D trajectory is an amazing journey. Enjoy your path. Go now! Here is to your beautiful arrival! This becomes the strategy you can implement when you are ready to live a life by design. To be on the forward edge of humanity assisting, designing and leading the way to what is possible.

The Eight Steps of Life By Design

- 1 **Owning Your Cognitive Dissonance (CD)** Coming to grasp with what is accurate to the best of your ability (The practice, as you develop your level of mastery here everything opens up). Differentiating what is so vs. what is not so. Observing the trap, this is where all your obstacles and stops come from. They live here. Evaluate the meaning of everything. "Our Collective **Un**consciousness; being out of alignment."

- 2 **De Cognitive Dissonance (DCD)** Recognition of your power to create. Differentiating your obstacles and removing your stops. Generating new interpretations which align with your optimal aptitude and abilities to propel you forward into your purpose and maximum contribution to humanity, your new life by design awaits. Suffering Index Gap (**SIG**) is the time it takes to go from CD to DCD. "Our Collective Consciousness; being in alignment"

- 3 **Cognitive Agility (CA)** Practicing **DCD** / **SIG** getting your hands on the wheel. Beginning to generate your own insights, distinctions and paradigms. Your creativity, imagination and confidence are increasing as you fill in the gaps. This is where life by design starts to take off.

- 4 **Integrating your Practice** into your body, mind and soul. Optimizing your system, becoming your best friend and increasing your self-value and love. This is where managing your well-being becomes your priority so you are nurtured and have the ability for maximum contribution. Being balanced allows for flow to happen.

- 5 **Defining your Purpose** By using the tools from your practice this far we explore your passions and dreams further so we are able to forward an optimal life by design strategy while having a practical look over the edge. We considering logistical issues and preparing for a beautiful landing.

- 6 **The Dimensional Bridge** Recognition of where you are on the bridge allows for fine tuning your life by design and making adjustments while being accountable, responsible and anticipating the unknown. You are fully aware of your purpose and your connection with the collective consciousness and the importance of your contribution to humanity.

- 7 **The Pause Principle Mastery of Mindfulness** You are on the bridge grounded and including everything (even your fears) with confidence. Standing on the edge you are **Jumping off the Edge Responsibly** into your gift.

- 8 **Elevate you Practice of Mastery** Continuing your integration while increasing your awareness and ability to access the Synchronicity and executing on your purpose. Sharing with others your growth and practice, being of service, preparing to jump off the next edge.

Jumping off the Edge Responsibly a Metaphor for your Cognitive Agility (**CA**) and our physical ability to adapt and change often and rapidly. Jumping off the edge responsibility allows you greater access to our universal knowledge and information which gives you greater access to remembering your unity and connectedness.

Some direct benefits, the life freedoms which are a result of doing what you love well, while being aligned with your purpose are as follow:

- 1 Abundance and financial freedom. Money is a consequence of doing what you love well. Our projects have magic when we are aligned.

- 2 Location freedom. Living where you belong and are connected.

- 3 Time to schedule and choose your project freedom. Using the digital world optimally to forward your projects and programs on your terms.

- 4 Who you want to work with freedom. Being aligned with the people who you work with, you elevate each other, bringing out optimal creativity and project implementation.

- 5 Your purpose freedom. You are in your zone, free to create, educate, inspire and teach others how to do the same. Contributing your gift.

I have a dream (MLK Reframe) that all people are created uniquely with their own specific gifts talents and aptitudes and that one day humanity and the unification of our common good will respect our equal rights for all mankind, regardless of our skin color, language, whether we are man or woman, or whatever our spiritual beliefs are, or our sexual preference may be. We the people have the right to use our imagination and creativity to generate new ideas, distinctions and paradigms to unify humanity, while retiring those old paradigms which are oppressive and have outlived their usefulness. Uniting ourselves through our common education, learning, freedom and bravery is our goal. We must be courageous since our global leadership is not having the success required for us to be sustainable on our planet. We need our movement to do the work for humanity. Be courageous and forward this movement for we the people by learning to include your fears and never being stopped by them in our pursuit of continuing to question everything which controls us or attempts to define us. We are a creation, a work in progress crossing the bridge together to a more connected future. A future which continues to define us newly as we grow and learn to contribute more efficiently to our global brothers and sisters and the quality of life on our planet. We have many edges to jump off before our work is done, and we will continue jumping off the edge responsibly, and peacefully to develop mastery in our cognitive agility and our ability to create sustainability for all. Our amazing world by design!

Continue Elevating your Practice of Mastery

Anyone who stops learning is old, whether at 20 or 80. Anyone who keeps learning stays young. The greatest thing in life is to keep your mind young. — *Henry Ford*

Chapter 11
Conclusions Life is Better with a Coach

As we continue to awaken as a species and forward our work in helping others to cross the bridge, it is our privilege to be of service to our fellow man. Continue elevating your practice of mastery and increasing your connection to your family, friends, coworkers and everyone else you may come in contact with. This is our ultimate resource of knowledge and wisdom. As you continue to open and develop your powerful relationship with mastery, your abilities will become more evident in your life by design. The purpose of your specific contribution will continue revealing the details that need to be implemented in the overall design of your amazing life dream. Helping others to eliminate their obstacles so they can make their contribution while sharing their unique gifts is a gift you give yourself. By helping others, you are reinforcing your own learning and ability to access deeper knowledge to apply to your projects success.

You must remain mindful of excessive reasonableness and how its meaning complicates your obstacles to the point of inaction. It is not the breakdown which is the problem as you may see it, it is the meaning you assign to the issue which is your obstacle or stop. Include your fears, stops and obstacles and do it anyway! Life is an experiential lesson to be lived. It is in the generation of alternate perspectives or meanings to your initial thoughts which puts your hands on the controls of your life by design. Integrating all the tools into your projects and life is freedom.

Crossing the Sustainability Bridge can happen as fast as you are willing to go. Continue minimizing the Suffering Index Gap (**SIG**).

- Some people are ready willing and excited to cross. They are wide open, anxious and awake. Practicing a high level of mastery with confidence, trusting the process and following their inspiration.

- Some people are ready and alert and, they are cautious and awake. Practicing their level of mastery with a sense of 'yea but.'

- Some people are willing yet have considerations, a degree of resistance, they are not yet free of their **CD** power rearing its ugly head. Most people are in this group. This is where we must continue to practice and assist others, so they are not stopped by the meanings they assign to their obstacles. The distinction of **SIG** and practicing the Pause Principle / Mastery of Mindfulness is key to identifying the specific obstacle and why it stops or restricts progress in any endeavor. Once you identify it, a solution is only a new insight, distinction, or perspective away. You are a paradigm generating machine, enjoy the process.

When I first started this practice, I loved helping people to realize their full potential and turn their perceived problems around. Watching the lights come on when they realize their new possibility; a path forward that had not occurred to them before. It is my continued pleasure and gift in helping individuals and organizations transform their dreams into reality. It is in being a person committed to our sustainability (physically, socially, culturally and spiritually) and doing my part in assisting others to cross the bridge, that is my expression of love and contribution to humanity.

I believe you are ready now, so jump into your gifts by scheduling a discovery session where we can speak to uncover, explore and assess your specific opportunity to move forward and begin implementing your life by design plan. Just go to my web site at **www.davidvletas.com** to schedule your free Discovery Session.

The Eight Steps to Life By Design will have you not be stopped by your obstacles any longer!

Chapter 12
Designing a Crossing the Bridge Plan

Being on the bridge is powerful, it is our access to looking forward and looking backward, while being grounded in the present. When we are being powerful and leading in the direction of our optimal contribution we are an unstoppable force of nature. I like to think of the dimensional bridge as The Bridge to our Sustainability for Humanity, the path forward for our fellow man to follow (physically, socially, culturally and spiritually).

When you want something, all the universe conspires in helping you to achieve it. — Paulo Coelho

Our confidence and abilities grow as we continue the practice, to increase our level of mastery across all domains. Using **The Pause Principle Mastery of Mindfulness** is a great tool to orient yourself when you are facing the challenges of life. Beginning with your outcome in mind is powerful and reminds you of how being your own best friend is important to your overall realization of your life by design. In this regard, the outcome is crossing the bridge and forwarding your projects while helping as many people as possible to the 5D / 21st Century future.

Utilizing your optimal aptitudes and skill sets to build your life dream is where your major achievements will occur. There is something about possibilities unfulfilled which are perhaps the most exciting thing we create. Sometimes we experience a let-down after a new project is implemented, that is our reality check in the present with our anticipation or expectations from the future removed. Embrace the process and continue being focused with conviction, including it all. One last point about being on the bridge, the power of the 5D pulling us across: This is our sustainable consciousness guiding us away from the 3D world and our old paradigms, and onto the 4D bridge. The Pause Principle Mastery of Mindfulness is a place to reflect what it is you are designing. Being pulled into your 5D future of the awakened paradigms. Once your practice is grounded in speaking **for** ideas, and free of the 3D ways of speaking **about** people or things, then your level of mastery is solid and you will be ready to engage your optimal strategy or project fully, you are unstoppable.

I am going to enjoy speaking with you so we may begin creating your life by design journey. I am committed to helping individuals and organizations excel in achieving the goals they are building. Our global network of consultants, coaches and trainers assist in increasing productivity, satisfaction and customer loyalty internationally.

If you would like additional information about how to implement these strategies please be in communication, or if you would like information regarding additional retreats, services or programs please contact me at:

Costa Rica Wellness Institute
Nosara, Costa Rica C.A.
David R. Vletas
E-mail: David@DavidVletas.com

Schedule your Discovery Session here:

www.davidvletas.com

If you would like to share a free copy of this book with a friend, you may go to the site below and send them one by entering their email.

Just let them know it will be on the way, so they will be looking for it.

www.JumpingOffTheEdge.com

The Strategic Intervention Coach's Oath

SEEK THE TRUTH

FIND EVERYONE FASCINATING

ALLOW YOURSELF THE HONOR OF
HUMILITY

KNOW THAT EVERY PERSON HAS A
SUPPORT SYSTEM

HELP THEM TO IMPROVE THEIRS

DO NO HARM

BE THE BRIDGE, THE ELEVATOR, AND
THE TRANSLATOR WHEN NEEDED

WEAR A SHERLOCK HOLMES HAT

BE YOURSELF FIRST AND ALWAYS

USE ANY AND ALL CONCEPTS TO HELP

ALL IDEAS, MODES, AND TRADITIONS
ARE WELCOME AND OF USE TO YOU

ALLOW FLOW AND CREATIVITY TO SET
YOU FREE

LET PAUSE, SILENCE AND REFLECTION
GIVE YOU STRENGTH

TREASURE THE INDIVIDUAL

BE UNIQUENESS UNFOLDING

CONTACT THE INNER VOICE AND THEN
INVITE IT TO CONVERSE

CREATE ACTIONS WHICH EMPOWER
CHANGE

FIND ROADS NOT TAKEN AND EXPLORE
THESE

EMBRACE YOUR OWN DOUBTS AND
DIFFICULT EMOTIONS

LISTEN AND ATTUNE

LET PURPOSE LEAD THE WAY

CREATE STRENGTH IN DOING

USE ACTIONS IN THE REAL WORLD
WHENEVER POSSIBLE

HONOR LOVE IN ALL ITS FORMS

LOOK FOR THE MEANING BENEATH
COMMUNICATIONS
ACCEPT WHAT IS AND EMBRACE WHAT
COULD BE
EXPLORE DECISIONS FROM THE PAST AS
OPPORTUNITIES TODAY
GIVE VOICE TO THE PARTS OF SELF IN
HIDING
SEE POSSIBILITY EVERYWHERE

Further Reading

The Difference Process

You Can Heal Your Life

A Course In Miracles

Who Moved My Cheese

The One Thing

Be Here Now

One Minute Mentoring

The Truth About Cancer

The Sacred Science

The Truth About Vaccines

Acknowledgement

The experience of working with the Author Castle and Dr. Angela Lauria including her solid team has been inspiring. The course design and materials are well thought out and professional. The most powerful part is in their approach and its divergence from traditional publishing. Dr. Lauria has the content and the message of her clients at heart and a chemistry exists between you and her when you have the pleasure of working with her. Her emphasis is on being the authors coach and guiding her clients in a way that has their message be heard, instead of traditional publishing's mantra of can we make money off your writing. Thank you for helping me write this book, without our synchronicity it would not have happened.

I am thankful to Landmark Education for initially capturing my attention, creativity and imagination and to truly setting me free to live the amazing life I have today. It has been an incredible ride and without some of the breakthroughs your work helped to facilitate, my life would have been much different. No amount of praise can convey my gratitude for the gifts I received through my training and development with Landmark. This is where I learned to be a mentor and a coach and the human being I am today. These are beautiful gifts we give to one another. I also wanted to give my special thanks to Werner Erhard, it was inspiring working with you at the Six Day and in San Francisco while watching the magic unfold.

I also want to give special thanks to Strategic Intervention (SI) coaching and specifically Magali and Mark Peysha for their mentoring and coaching, which continues to this day. Everyone benefits from having a coach and or mentor. You are both an inspiration to me in your own unique ways and a source of much strength. Thank you for being the rock and having my back. If ever I need anything, I know you are there. It is always a pleasure watching you coach while giving everything you have to forward your clients growth. Your patience and willingness to be with difficult situations is exemplary, for us all, and your truly amazing contribution to humanity.

Last, I would like to acknowledge all my family, friends, coworkers, clients and the beautiful souls I quoted in this book. We have shared our life experiences together. I am who I am because of you, and I thank you. Finally,

I want to say thank you to my partner Kathryn, who is my best friend and example of how great a person can be. I love you all.

Author Biography

David R. Vletas is the CEO of Eagle Production Inc., a global consulting firm. EPI designs and implements initiatives to elevate individuals, families and organizational performance. It is in our satisfaction and an overall mindfulness for life where we connect to our optimal aptitudes for contribution. Vletas has worked with over a thousand people since 1992 mentoring and coaching them to produce transformational results in their lives. EPI is also in the energy sector being a bridge to a less hydrocarbon dependent society. Our sustainable future, and one focused on renewable resources are increasingly important for the planet. We are in an "Energy Renaissance" increasing our individual abilities and our technological efficiencies. Our connection to humanity is our most valuable resource.

Vletas has a deep respect and love of the oceans with surfing being his passion. It is through our individual connection with nature, which is one of our unifying forces and more important than most of us realize. As our awareness increases around this issue we will be propelled towards the required paradigm shifts necessary for humanity's sustainability. This is our purpose and focus, bringing this awakening to individuals and organizations globally. Doing what inspires your contribution is key.

Vletas attended Colorado School of Mines in Golden, and the University of Texas at Austin where he received a BS in Geology with a minor in petroleum engineering. He has done extensive training and development work with Landmark Education where he was an Introduction to the Forum Leader. Vletas is also a Strategic Intervention Coach and continues to train and develop himself in the Master Level Coach Training Mentorship Program. Vletas is committed to helping individuals and organizations in achieving an extraordinary Life By Design experience and results. By designing individually or with your multidisciplinary team and while implementing whatever we define as missing to forward the progress of any project. Both practically and creatively moving forward your collective vision. Vletas lives in Costa Rica with his partner, Kathryn and their amazing dog, Mango. Jumping Off The Edge Responsibly is an Amazon #1 Best Seller.

The Best is Yet to Come!

Some of the Companies I have worked with:

Exxon / Cogdell Field / Kent County, Texas

Texaco / Doward Field / Scurry & Garza Counties, Texas

Anadarko / Sharron Ridge Field / Scurry County, Texas

UPRC / Green River Formation / Green River, Wyoming

Sun Oil Company / Howard County Acquisitions, Texas

Bridwell Oil Company / Eastern Shelf Properties, Texas

Retamco / Penn. Play / Nolan & Fisher Counties, Texas

Foree Oil Company / Penn. Play / Runnels, Nolan & Fisher Counties Texas

Encon Services / City Services / Eastern Shelf, Texas

Rhodes Drilling / Grissom Field & Griffin Ranch / Haskel & Taylor Counties Texas

Polk & Patton / Eastern Shelf Prospects / Texas

Elco Oil & Gas / Pecan Station Field / Tom Green County, Texas

3-M Energy / Permian Basin Projects / Martin, Reagan, Irion Counties, Texas

Barlow & Haun / Wyoming Projects / Green River County, Wyoming

Gillespie Exploration / Canyon Sand Development / Jones County, Texas

EC Tool & Supply / Holley Ellenberger & Strawn Sand Field / Nolan & Fisher County, Texas

Spalding Energy / San Andres Projects / Scurry County, Texas

Allegro Operating / Eastern Shelf Operations
& Acquisitions / Texas

Henley Oil & Gas / Palo Pinto Study / Easter
Shelf, Texas

Mel Richards Oil / Ellenberger Study / Nolan
& Fisher Counties, Texas

Harken Oil & Gas / Eastern Shelf Prospects /
Texas

Le Clair Operating / Penn Study / Runnels
County, Texas

Solar Exploration / Griffen Ranch Project /
Taylor & Colemen Counties, Texas

J&J Services / Penn Study / Runnels, Concho,
Tom Green, Meanard, Irion & Schleicher
Counties, Texas

Mid-Energy / Williams Ranch Study /
Schleicher & Irion Counties, Texas

Capstone Innovations / Wolfcamp & Canyon
Sand Play / Schleicher County, Texas

JD Oil & Gas / Hatchell Field Development /
Runnels County, Texas

Pearson Siebert / Iatan East Howard Field
Area / Howard County, Texas

Paul Barwis / Geophysical Projects /
Schleicher County, Texas

Clearfork Operating / Red Cave Gas Project /
Baca County, Colorado

Ray Moss & Elizabeth Halliburton / Mineral
Appraisal, Revenue in Suspense Retrieval /
Oklahoma & Texas

**We are the bridge to a less
hydrocarbon dependent society.
Generating our new sustainable
energy paradigm together
Physically, Socially, Culturally and
Spiritually
We are all capable of designing
a more magnificent life than we can
imagine!**

www.DavidVletas.com

Notes ~

Notes ~

Notes ~

Notes ~

Notes ~

Notes ~

Notes ~

Notes ~

Notes ~

Notes ~

Notes ~